Broken Pages

Poetic prose for the broken soul

Papikins

Cyrus Ahmadnia

Papikins

Broken Pages

Copyright © 2021 by Cyrus Ahmadnia (Papikins)

All rights reserved. No part of this book may be reproduced in any form or by any electronic or mechanical means, including information storage and retrieval systems, without permission in writing from the publisher, except by a reviewer who may quote brief passages in a review.

This book is a creative work of non-fiction, which has been derived from various experiences and observations. However, some instances have been created from the imagination.

ISBN 978-1-9168832-0-8 (Paperback)

ISBN 978-1-9168832-1-5 (eBook)

Published by Papikins Publishing

www.papikins.com

Cover designer

Gabriel Akinrinmade

www.boxofwolves.com

Papikins

Broken Pages

This is for those who hurt in silence.

You will forever be my unwritten masterpiece.

Papikins

Table of contents

The broken	1
This is for you	2
The person I once knew	6
Hurt together	11
The romantic	16
Broken smile	20
Blinded	24
Save us from dying	25
Holding on to lies	27
The void you left me with	28
Pedestal	31
Face without a name	32
Romance is dead	34
Heal together	40
Inept	45
The catalyst	53
Behind this skin	56
Wasting breath on you	59
The victim	63
The villain	64

Broken Pages

The saviour	65
The witness	66
Friendship fades	67
Damsel in distress	71
Gaslight	77
The fear of yesterday	80
The lies I tell myself	84
Monster	87
The fall	88
A hundred days	91
Until my breath escapes me	93
My heart bleeds blue	95
Just breathe	101
Broken pages	102
Distractions	103
Beyond my broken crown	107
The king of the broken	114
Entirety	119

The broken

My name is Papikins, and I apologise in advance if any of this hurts. I just want us to connect. I want to show you why they call me the broken artist. I want to be your saviour, as I eventually play the victim and the villain. These are the stories of regret that somehow faded off into the distance. You see, everything is temporary. We fight to be relevant in a place where nothing stays the same. We breathe and we break. We love and we ache. It's a shared story that most of us will go through, and I sincerely hope I do it justice, not just for me, but for you – the silent one who reads this.

We are the broken. We're the truth behind the lies that we've been told. We desperately yearn for validation, as our hearts are torn by a thousand reasons. These are the chapters that haunt us to no end. I always wanted to connect without the fear of being censored, and here I am with these broken pages. I hope you enjoy my poetic prose for the broken soul. This is me in all my glory. This is me in my entirety. These are the reasons why my heart bleeds blue.

Broken Pages

This is for you

I'm an overthinker, and maybe you are too. We wouldn't share this moment if we had nothing in common. You see, a thousand words echo through my head to calm me from my nerves. I keep thinking, and I keep thinking until I overthink. I wander all across my mind to find the pieces I somehow left behind. It's sad. It really is. We adapt to those around us, suppressing who we are inside, until we're a scattered soul without a home. This is Papikins. This is Cyrus. This is me in my entirety. This is my journey. This is everything I've felt and done, but the worst is yet to come. These are the words that have ripped my heart in two, as it bleeds a broken shade of blue. I'm the victim, the villain, and the saviour. It's the hardest part to handle. Throughout our lives we're viewed from many angles, and most of us are perceived as someone we may or may not be. It depends on the eyes that scan our insecurities.

    I've been labelled as the villain more than I can count. I never seem to understand why I'm the one at fault. I'm restlessly in love with the idea of human nature, because we seamlessly place the blame on others. It's how we move the world around us. We wear masks to decrease our chances of rejection, because we fear we may not be accepted. It's how it is to be the victim. You constantly regret the flaws that you've been hiding until suddenly you're alone again. It's bound to happen. You lower your defences, not knowing that you're vulnerable without them. The truth is you have to save yourself rather than rely on someone else.

Some of us fail to understand that emotions are like travellers. We slyly move around the hurt, not letting it all out. We fall into distractions to remove all of our doubts. I never knew what I was doing until I took some time to think, and believe me, I thought a large amount. I wanted to be connected to all these pretty pictures that flew around inside my mind. I wanted to catch the stars and somehow steal their shine. Sadly, there was nothing I could do to stop myself from falling. I guess you have to fall sometimes to remember who you are. I never meant to change, but that's part of life that many of us despise. We have a fear of letting go of a past that burns us without fire. We're afraid of the unwritten, because the chapters may lead us to somewhere foreign.

There's a sadness to the world that most of us avoid. We want to be happy when happiness isn't close to what we need. I'm no different when it comes to being human. I have this desire for my words to be my version of almost perfect, yet I know that they'll never reach it. I always wonder what it's like to be a different person. I never enjoy the smaller things, because I'm in a constant state of thinking. My mind is made of moments, yet all I do is focus on the broken. Maybe it's the reason why I'm like this. I'm fascinated by my feelings, or I used to be at least. I wanted to find the reasons why I'm hurting, and if I'll ever feel enlightened, but sadly, that part of me is dead. I was slightly fixated on wanting to find myself beyond the mask I'm wearing, but unluckily, I found a broken mess.

There were a thousand chapters in my life, or that's how it seemed to feel. I kept going in circles, trying to find myself after every ending. It isn't easy starting over. You build the characters and settings until they stop existing. It's the reason why we can barely overcome a broken heart. We're not used to pain. We try to avoid it at all costs. We're the broken beings of yesterday, because we never seem to live within today. We're stuck inside the past to heal the part of us that never seemed to last. It's the saddest truth when it comes to overthinking. We focus too much on what used to be rather than what is.

I would always look at the stars to find peace, but all I ever did was turn them into dust. It's how my mind works at times. I stare at something for so long with a million different thoughts and suddenly they're gone. I guess it's the human side of me that prevents me from remotely being anywhere close to happy. I stopped believing in happiness a long time ago. I couldn't bear to handle it, because it made me feel lesser than I usually do. It never appealed to me after my heart began to bleed in blue. That's how the world is. It takes you from point to point, as it breaks apart your sanity. We experience love and loss without ever realising that it could

Broken Pages

happen to us. That's why it's unexpected. That's why these faces fade away whenever we hope to stay the same. I'm sorry if this hurts you but hurt is part of life. I wanted to surround myself with beauty yet found it hard to control the broken side of me. We can never control our thoughts as fully as we want to. We're bound to fall a thousand times as we drown within the boundaries of our lives. It happens to the best of us. Believe me, I know it.

I'm an overthinker that ruins everything around them. I used to blame it on my thoughts, because I never had control. I still have many flaws, but I've been trying to get better. I have this craving for attention, and no matter how much I think that I'm adored, I still have the need for more. It's weird, isn't it? I want to be loved yet want to be alone. I want the world to know me behind the skin I live in, but I prefer to sit here on my own. Is it wrong to feel like I'm disconnected? Is it wrong to want to be somebody else? Someone loved and not neglected? It's the same story, isn't it? You know me, and I know you. We're miles apart, but you somehow feel this. Congratulations, you've let me in. I hope I can make you feel less lonely. I truly do. This isn't just for me; this is for you.

Broken Pages

The person I once knew

Love and loss come hand in hand like yin and yang. They complement one another as we somehow feel two extremes at once. I wish everything was simple. I wish I could tell you that love is never-ending, but the reality is that heartbreak is forever trending. It happened to me, it's possibly happened to you, and it may happen once again. That's how life is when it comes to being lonely. You want to find a purpose, so you let go of all your senses. There's this drive to feel as though you're needed, but in reality, you're a broken shell of who you used to be. Believe me, I've felt it. I've chased for reasons why these waves would fill me with discontent as they crashed into the shore. I thought that I'd resurface, but I changed into a person that I never knew before.

    I'm sorry if this isn't what you expected it to be. I want to share these broken pages that are made up of my story. I want to let you in and be the one who saves you from the madness. It may be wrong to feel like this, but suddenly words escape my breath that ashamedly make sense. I've tried to change my style of thinking, but the resistance made it hard for me to find acceptance. I was always far away and dreaming, yet I never allowed myself to do exactly what I wanted. I couldn't achieve anything, or maybe I could, but I just refused to see it. My self-esteem has always been my downfall. It's the part of me I hate the most. There are days where I feel invincible, but there are others where I disconnect from everything I know. I'm my own worst enemy at times, especially when there's no one else around. I just want to stop these thoughts from ruining me, because they seem to flow into my veins and strip me of my dignity.

I was begging for change, but I was too far gone to actually be saved. I never wanted to admit that I could be the problem, but suddenly I saw the world from views that were out of my perception. I saw so many flaws that I refused to witness, as I dismantled the parts of me that were full of sadness. I knew that I was different, or maybe it was me who only thought so. I felt a shiver down my spine as I walked around sedated. I would stare at my reflection and wonder why I'm full of wrong decisions. I was scared of my appearance, because all I ever saw were bloodshot eyes and a broken heart. I knew that love was part of my demise, and it seemed to kill me deep inside. It's always love that's on my mind. I used to believe that it could brighten up my life, but the truth was somewhat different. It's the reason why I feel so fucking distant.

The moon was the only light I knew as my mind was racing to find answers old and new. Why am I alone, and why am I still hurting? I kept thinking, and I kept thinking until my mind was breaking. It was the only option I had to find clarity within my self-destruction. I wanted to close this chapter of my story with a smile rather than the tears that kept on flowing. I thought about love relentlessly, trying to make sense of what is real and what is fiction. There was no escape from this dreaded feeling. I was afraid of falling deep within a web of lies that I created. I tried to play the victim, not realising that I should take the blame instead. I wanted to transfer it, because I was scared I would hate myself again. It was hard to understand it, as I pushed myself to be submissive. These vulnerabilities began to seep through the cracks my heart was trying to repair. I was looking for protection in a place where my sanity was questioned. I was living through the past rather than learning to embrace the present.

The truth is that there were days where I would succumb to overthinking, and I would put myself into restless situations. I was searching for resurgence, as I put myself at risk of fading. I was ashamed of even breathing, as I wallowed in self-loathing. I wanted to disappear, as my heart shattered into pieces. I knew loneliness was looming around the corner and I tried my best not to greet it. This is how it is to love and to lose. We can barely control our emotions, as we find ourselves drawn to heartbreak and mistakes. We want to be simplistic, so we aim to see the world as narrow, but refuse to realise that there are more souls out there for us to value.

I had this idea that souls were meant to be together, but the world is cruel in ways that are hard to fathom. We feel as though we lose our chance when our hearts begin to crack. It's as if no one else exists other than the one who hurt you, so you fall, and you fall, and you keep falling until there's nothing left. There's a problem with being human. We lose track of everything around us, as we fall victim to a blurring of our vision. We only see that one person yet refuse to believe there are others out there who can heal us. We attach ourselves to nothing and ultimately push away our dreams. It's what we do when we're caught up in our emotions. We aim for instant gratification yet fear for the worst when it never happens.

I was a firm believer of the beauties within love and how it should be treated like an art. There comes a time when you lose yourself to a point where you're unrecognisable, and you begin to see it differently. You feel as though you're cursed, as you wonder why this beautiful feeling ends in hurt. I was constantly trying to pour my heart into these pages, and these words would formulate a past that I could never manage. My mental health was suddenly declining, as I became addicted to the sensation of ink running down my fingers. I wanted to release every single feeling. I wanted to be heard as long as I'm still breathing.

I was running from these memories that made me senselessly look for something better. I wanted to erase the past I felt before, yet never knew to what extent that I would fall, and believe me, I felt like I was drowning. I was deep within the blue, resisting all these demons that crept into my view. I swam up to the surface with no recollection of what it meant to be an individual. I was focused on regaining the love I lost, as I tried to make it through. I didn't feel like I was anything more than less, and that was the final straw to my fight with loneliness. I was so empty. I could feel a tight grip around my throat. It was suffocating everything I worked for. I couldn't breathe at all. I was hoping someone would save me, but sadly, I had to save myself. It's hard, you know?

Broken Pages

Putting yourself in a position to be this open. I surrendered to these thoughts of love and loss, as I tried to gain control. I wanted to remember every single detail. I wanted to finally be real. It was a breaking point that changed the way I live, because it turned me into a broken mess of brokenness.

I was tired of being just another face. I wanted people to see me beneath this human skin. I combed through every hope and dream to get a sense of what it was that I was missing. I had to stop dreaming and start becoming. I never felt enough until I saw beauty behind my sadness. I knew I was meant for more. I had to expose myself completely. I knew that in the end, everything would be meaningless with time. We refuse to see life the way it is. We let the minutes pass, not realising that years are slowly wasted, and that's exactly why I had to give up on the fears that held me hostage.

I had to build my walls back up from the ground. I stared out into space and saw a lack of understanding to being afflicted by depression. I felt a lock around my chest, as the world was slightly spinning. I wondered if anyone else felt the way I do, and surprisingly, I was never as alone as I had thought. I naturally connected to other people. They needed me. They needed hope without dishonesty. I had to be the voice for all these shattered souls, as I tried to set alight the world with poetry and prose. It was part of my transition to becoming the king of the broken. I played the victim and the villain when I was meant to be the saviour. I'll repeat it one last time; this is for you, the person I once knew.

Hurt together

You look beautiful tonight, like you always do. I'm sorry the world has been a little crazy, but hasn't it always been? We never want to see it. We never want to admit that everything is fucked, from humanity to reality. We sugar-coat the lies to make them taste a little sweeter, but we end up losing hope that tomorrow will somehow be a little better. I want us to hurt together. I've said it time and time again, but sometimes, you have to repeat words to make people stay. You have to say, 'I love you' or even a simple 'hey'. You see, everything is simplistic, and I'm simply just poetic. I've seen the sadness behind your eyes and they still make me feel like I'm alive. I'm in love with you. I'm in love with the stranger that's reading this. I know you're slightly just confused, but we force ourselves to love based on assumptions that we create. You're beautiful, so fucking beautiful, and I really wish the best for you, but here we are, sharing a different kind of pain.

There are so many words I wish that I could say, just to make you smile again. I wonder if it'll be a perfect shape or if your lips will crumble as they quake. I know you. I know you so well that I am you. We fake a smile to feel as though we're happy, but where was happiness when our worlds were slowly breaking? I want you to let me in. I need you to, because this is how it starts when you fall in love with a dream. You let go of your intuitions and let yourself fall back into another's arms. I want us to hurt together, so badly. I want to lift you up and bring you down, just like every other story. You're perfectly aligned with the stars that exist within your mind, yet here you are, trying to decode each and every line. I'm sorry. I'm so sorry that every word forms into a conversation, but I want you to feel me more than you've ever felt anyone before. I need you to.

I know you've faced a war within yourself, and I'm attracted to your agony. I love that side of you, because it formed you in your entirety. We always want to erase our misery, leaving chapters without an end, but why? Why would we want to let go of who we are? There are times where we have nothing left at all, but as we learn to grow, we push aside the hate and show our scars to prove that we were brave. We never seem to realise that life is made of hurt. We go through stages of regret, and we're in denial when trying to forget. It's a harsh truth to being broken. Fuck. You're such a beautiful distraction. I can feel you reading this, and I'm speechless. That's the thing about connection. I can sense you in my mind, as I traverse the universe. I hope these words make sense, because I'm unsure of what this is. I guess I'm cursed to be a broken artist.

The worst is always yet to come. We place our trust in everyone, or so it feels. We want them to believe we're worth their time and energy, but they won't. The truth is that most of us neglect ourselves in hopes that others will see us clearly.

Broken Pages

No one will ever see you if you refuse to see yourself. I realised that a long time ago. I would always put myself last because I was scared that I could never amount to much. I never felt enough. I was tired of who I was, but I never truly knew myself. It's sad. It really is. We hate ourselves the most when we barely understand. I find it to be destructive. I know you do it too. Don't lie to me. I know you stare at your reflection, wishing you were a different person. Do you even know yourself to begin with? I kept thinking, and I kept thinking until my mask had fallen.

We devalue ourselves as time goes on. We see our flaws too vividly to stay strong. We want to stop breathing for a second, but all we do is hurt without a reason. I want us to hurt together. I need us to. I need you to understand that everything you feel is made to tear you into pieces. We do it to ourselves. We create this false belief that happiness is what we need, when in reality, we're aiming for perfection. Nothing is perfect. We hide the truth with insincerity, as we scour through our story to find a glimpse of hope that we'll one day reach our goals. We set them too high to begin with, focusing on love and comparisons between fabricated lifestyles. I wish I could tell you that everything will be fine, but it won't.

I don't want to be someone who lies to you. I don't want to make you feel good when you shouldn't. There will be days where darkness comes around, but it leaves as quickly as it came. That's the hardest part about life. We go through the motions, witnessing the moments. We always emphasise the negatives, as they linger in the air, causing us distress. We're affected by everything around us, as we try our best to smile. I'm addicted to your smile, even if I may not know you. I'm sorry. I seem to have lost myself within a stranger. It's how we are when we want to avoid the truth. We hide behind other people, even if we barely know them, but the truth is I feel like you're familiar. I feel like we've met before somewhere out there in the cold. We hurt a thousand times over yet always feel alone. I don't want to be alone anymore. I don't want to be alone with myself. I want us to hurt together.

You see, we're a lonely kind of species. We pray for someone to come into our lives and whisk us off our feet. We crave it, don't we? It's as if we're destined to want to fill the void. There have been times where I've wanted to disappear, but I'd only be running from myself. I've always been a monster. Maybe not to you, but it's all I see staring back at me inside the mirror. I sometimes go into a state of panic, wondering where all of my time went. It's the problem with being human. You want to watch the world burn until the ashes settle down. You think they'll wash away the hurt, but all they do is amplify the pain. I want you to hurt with me, because all of it is temporary. I want to feel your sadness, as the tears roll down your tender cheeks. I want to be your saviour, even if you perceive me as the villain.

Broken Pages

I always utter the worst is yet to come, but I understand that what I feel at this moment will be a memory. I've felt too many feelings and I've felt like I was at my lowest each and every year, but here I am still standing. Sometimes, we have to face the truth to come out better. We always assume the worst, but we miss out on a life we should have lived. We fear too much to actually exist. I'm never quite sure where I'm going. I coast from time to time, pretending that I'm living. I told you, I would never lie to you. I still feel uneasy, even when I'm thinking. I just want to get out all these thoughts before I find myself in shambles. I'm broken. I'm beaten. I'm borderline at best.

There will never be a perfect time. We lie to ourselves to make everything seem fine. Life is full of setbacks that repeatedly occur, and when they do, we find ourselves attacked. The problem is that we set our walls too high and never let them down again. We're too discouraged to find meaning, and it never seems to end. I want us to hurt together. I want you to understand what it is to live within the present. I want to seal away the cracks inside your heart after I tear it all apart. I want you to feel every word until you heal, and when you heal, I want you to think of me. I want you to remember everything I told you, because in the end, the only thing that matters is that you did it by yourself. I never had a chance to give you hope, because I was never really there.

The romantic

I believe in love. I believe that everything was made to be, but still your face is haunting me. It's hard to retain the memories. I retrace the past and what it did to me. I wanted it to be perfect, you know? I wanted to be whole. It's what we seem to do when we hate ourselves. It happens. We become attached too easily, unknowingly. We say 'I love you' within a whisper without sound. We mouth the words like magic, hoping to be found. We never seem to care about who we tell those special words to, because we hope for the best, as long as our hearts are beating within our chests. We want connection. We want to be a slave to the system. We write these notes of happiness to feel a little less. It's distracting, I guess. We always want to be the centre of attention, but somehow, we have to fight to stay important. That's the harsh truth when it comes to being with another person. You have to keep them entertained, or suddenly, they fade into another memory.

We have this complicated reason why we seem to hurt. We forget about what it means to be connected, so our stories seem to drift away. The ones we hold close turn from strangers into lovers, but in the end, they always leave a burn. We think we're owed the world whenever we connect. We feel as though we're supposed to flourish, but the truth is that we break at the faintest sight of failure. I would always give

Broken Pages

too much, yet still seemed to fall apart. I was stuck inside forever, not realising that it's just a dream. You see, when you're an overthinker, you hold on to every missing piece, trying to attach them back together. You suddenly become aware of mistakes that left you speechless. Your thoughts become an unruly addiction, as you think, and you think until you overthink to a point of no return. It took me a while to see it, but these thoughts of you were all I ever had. I wanted to understand. I wanted to bring you back. That was my problem. I should have kept on walking. We stand still for too long when we're in pain. We find it hard to move, but the truth is that our minds have been infected.

I thought there was nothing I could do to erase these memories of you. I was only hurting myself with questions of why you left, but it's life, I guess. You were every word inside my head. You occupied the depths of me that I never wanted to let free. You were part of my story, and I wouldn't change anything about what happened. That's what all of us ever seem to do. We want to change our history. We want to remove the love we lost because we're scared to face reality. It's the same story repeatedly. We're afraid to be alone, so we force ourselves to hide away the yesterday that we adored. I distanced myself from everyone. I didn't want them to see the side of me that made me feel so small. I just wanted to feel better by myself. It's what we do to appear strong. We refuse to let others see us weak, so we hide, and we hide until there's nothing left to store. I wanted to disappear, I guess. I wanted to find a way out of this mess. It wasn't all about love. It was about the idea of being alone without trust.

You sometimes fall into the void, and you seem to forget how to form connections. You feel paranoid and lost. You treat the world more cautiously, because you have no idea what went wrong. It's the saddest part of heartbreak. We assume the worst is over when it's only just begun. It's love, isn't it? We value it too much but when it's gone, it hurts like hell to be alone. I've never felt that way before. I never understood why I was running out of fuel. The truth is always simple, yet we complicate our lives to keep ourselves happier than usual. We pave the way for restless nights to tangle up our souls and fill our minds with hurtful thoughts. I was always hopelessly in love. I always wanted what I saw in movies, but sadly, I never saw what's left after the credits ceased their scrolling. You somehow fade. You somehow let what used to be slowly but surely die, and it's hard. It really is. The moments turn to hate until suddenly it's over.

Where do we go from there? We learn what it means to be together, but we also learn what it means to be pulled apart. It's a cycle that never seems to end. We portray the loss of love like we were destined to forever lose our smiles. It isn't like that. We love and we lose. We lose and we love. We repeat it throughout our lives. There's always someone for everyone, yet we're blind. We're blinded by heartache because it's too much for us to take. We have a moment where

Broken Pages

we never let anyone in, because we're scared to hurt all over again. It's the worst kind of mindset to be in. We never want to give as much as we gave before, so we lock ourselves inside the stories that we told. I'm sorry if I hurt you, but these words are all I know. I repeat them back every single day, as I wonder where my mind will go.

It takes a lot of strength to find yourself again. I pushed aside my anger and made all these memories mine. I couldn't bear to stare at anything I lost until I found acceptance amidst the chaos. You can either keep on falling or breathe the air that you've neglected. I love the idea of love. I love the idea of belonging to someone that shows promise, but sadly, I hate the outcome. We're meant to stay together until our stories end. We may not even go back to being friends, but that's how the cookie crumbles. I realised that I never saw my worth, as I only seemed to stumble. I hated who I was after being torn apart, but that's how it is when you have a broken heart. The only thing that's certain is that time will somehow heal you. Memories are more precious than any of us know. The truth is you were beautiful with love, and you're still the same person that you supposedly had lost.

Broken smile

She was the sun, while I was the moon, and without her, I was left in the dark. I felt too much, too soon. She was a star that lit my lonely nights. I was mesmerised by her soul and by her grit, even though she was distant at times. She was the better part of me in a life full of tragedy, and as the days drew closer to our demise, I knew love like ours was never easy to find. Would I call it love or infatuation? I'm not quite sure how to define the difference. She was a ray of light, destined to make me shine. I wouldn't be here without her, even if I regret what happened sometimes. I wished for the best, but all I could conjure was a moment of stress. We fought beside one another until our hearts began to break within silence. She was imperfect yet so fucking worth it.

Whenever I would see her, she would somehow leave me breathless. I couldn't understand it, as we walked around without a sense of purpose. We were too far gone, too soon. She was everything that I ever needed, but all I ever did was create space between us. You see, this is why I'm lonely. I make decisions based on assumptions and watch everything burn around me. It's the hardest part to deal with when you lose yourself in thinking, and when I think, these thoughts push me deeper to the blue, as I slowly start to sink. I was only trying to be better than I was before, but eventually these walls I built around us began to crumble. We were drifting apart more than I could handle. It isn't easy to stare at something that you're losing. I could never seem to turn our pages back. I guess it's a part of life that makes us powerless. I wanted to fix our mistakes but created more of a mess.

The worst is always yet to come, and when you lose in love, you're left there torn in half. What a beautiful feeling yet so tragic at times. We deserve more than what we have but all we seem to do is fall for the same routine. I know you've felt it too. You've been in situations which only hurt your pride. You fell too hard, too soon. You wanted to make a world for two, but your heart suddenly got fucked, and now you bleed a shade of blue. It's sad, isn't it? We live for moments yet they only seem to haunt us. We're unable to let go of anything. We're tired of feeling low and defenceless, so we try to cut our losses. The truth is that our thoughts are baseless.

I would fill my head with pain, just to relive it all again. I wanted to be saved, but nothing could save me from the cycle. You see, I kept thinking, and I kept thinking until the sun was rising. The nights would pass me by, as I laid there trying not to close my eyes. I never wanted to let go. I never wanted to believe that I was made to be alone. There wasn't anything that I could do to stop myself from drowning, and believe me, I would have if I could. I saw the truth one day, as these memories slowly slipped away. She was everything, but only in my head. You become accustomed to people. You attach yourself to their souls and addiction starts to form. We never realise that when we're searching for answers. We hate to give logic to our suffering, so we create scenarios instead. They only do us harm, as we fill ourselves with doubt.

Stories like ours were never meant to be heard. I felt a spark every moment that our hands would lock together. I wish I could have told her that I wanted to be her saviour, but sometimes, we turn into the villain without ever even knowing. We were only going nowhere. I wish she would have seen me behind the skin I live in, but none of it seemed to ever matter. She was beautifully flawed, and that's what drew me into her. Perfection is unattainable, but her imperfections were all that I adored. She was indecisive yet defiant. She knew the words to say, even when we stood in silence. She was the girl with the broken smile. I feared for the worst every single night, as she locked away her pain. I found her to be enchanting in ways that made little sense at all. She was my everything, like I said before.

There are times where we find ourselves in people, and we're somehow attracted to the familiar likeness that's emitted. We want them to be our new beginning, and we'd move the world to have them there beside us. Is it love though? What is love? We define it so differently. Does it have any meaning left when no one can agree? It's sad but true. I was in love with the idea that she'd fall into my arms, but I forgot reality existed. I was living in a dream where she would finally be happy, somewhere out there, hopefully with me. We have too many feelings that cause our stories to conclude, sometimes unnaturally. I was caught up in the moment as most of us should be. There will always be that one person, or maybe two, or maybe more. That's the beautiful thing about acceptance. You realise that every chapter is made of a life that you once lived, until finally you're left with memories of a person you once knew.

Blinded

We were beautiful from whatever I recall. I could even say we had it all, but I'd be lying to myself. I used to turn a blind eye to the present to live out in a dream. It's all we ever were. We were a thought inside my head, when in reality our love would be better off as dead. I'd take our saddest moments and lock them up instead. I only wanted what was best. The thought of losing you was always out of the question. I was scared of what would happen if I was the only one who's left. I was selfishly in love with the secrets that I kept. I was hiding all our pain, hoping that we'd stay the same. It was never my intention to give you all that you could take, but as the days passed, I had to lose myself and break.

You lit fires with wood and stone, as you kept me burning through a love that made me feel so cold. You were etched into my skin, and I felt you everywhere I went. I was controlled by your hands that never felt as loving as I had hoped. I was at a point where I could hardly see my worth. I could only see the person that you left behind. I could only feel an emptiness that prevented me from loving life. It happens, I guess. I wanted to believe I found my missing piece, but only blinded myself to keep my mind at peace.

Save us from dying

We'll never be the same again. How does that feel? I'm not too sure. I saw you for who you are, and I didn't like what I was seeing. It's a shame that I was the only one trying to save us from dying. I thought you'd give me reasons to keep all of this together, but you were slowly fading as our love was getting weaker. I could see what was happening to us yet found it hard to leave. I was scared of letting go of the possibility of finally being happy. It's funny how everything comes together yet falls apart within an instant. We were playing with these strings that held both of us so distant. We could never cross a certain point, because we were focused on our different visions.

That's the sad part about being the only one who cared. I was always looking for a way to fix us, but apparently, we were broken beyond repair. I would have died for you, and that's the saddest truth. I wanted the best for us, even if you never felt it. I was always there whenever I could be, but I guess it wasn't enough to make you love me. I had a theory that one person stays in love while the other easily moves on, but now I've changed my mind. I drove myself to madness, as I constantly thought about your face and the plans we had before this. My world was shattering. I knew that our love had died, but I had hope that you'd bring me back to life. I wanted to save us from dying, but I only killed my self-belief. These are the days where I miss you. I thought everything would be perfectly fine, yet here I am with a broken smile and these thoughts of us. Where did we go wrong, and at what point did we begin to die? I've felt the pain of love, and now I stand as one. Is this how every story ends? We were so close, and now we're incapable of being friends. I wish that we could somehow go back to what we had, but it feels so distant now.

You were such a beautiful distraction. You took every worry that I had and hid it all away. It's why I loved you. You made me feel like I wasn't me. Maybe I was wrong to feel too strongly. Maybe I should have loved myself more to gain the courage to let you go. It's how we are when we fall in love. We unexpectedly begin to change. We leave behind our intuitions, as we start a brand new page. I wanted our chapter to be beautiful, but we ended a little too soon. It was the push I needed to see the world in blue, especially after you. I never understood why we weren't made to be forever. I thought that was how these fairy tales ultimately worked. I realised I wanted to be the saviour for a love that was destined for only failure.

Holding on to lies

Are you afraid? Why wouldn't you be? This is where we fall apart. I gave everything I had to make you see me, but it was never enough. You only saw the weakest parts that I displayed. You made me feel like I was crazy. You opened up my eyes and closed them simultaneously. I couldn't breathe or find a way to leave. I was addicted to the pain. I wanted to stay, even though I knew that we were going nowhere. It's funny, isn't it? I already knew that we had died, but never wanted to admit it. I wanted to be clueless, so I would hurt a little less, I guess.

We were hopelessly romantic, even when it ended. We were holding on to nothing until our heartache was extended. I had a thousand dreams that we would last a lifetime, but that's all they ever were, a dream of us together, going in these circles that never really mattered. Somehow, it feels like a memory that I never owned. It's as if this story belongs to someone else, and I'm observing from afar. It's upsetting that we never saw it through until the end, but sometimes people break apart. You were the only constant in this circle that I call life, but I guess the truth is that I was holding on to lies.

Broken Pages

The void you left me with

I walk around familiar places that we used to visit, wondering how to act when you and I had once existed. There's a void you left me with that's toying with my existence. It's as if these holes were made to amplify this emptiness I'm feeling. The streets are filled with memories, and I somehow feel you close to me. It's the little things I miss that make my heart feel cold. You'd always give me hope, yet little did I know that you would be the reason why I broke. I attached myself to misery just to rid your name and face from what I used to be. It hurts, you know. You put everything you have into love, but it never goes as planned. I was tired of looking back. I was afraid this void would somehow turn my heart to black, but the worst was yet to come. I bled in the colour of an ocean, and these thoughts of drowning were all I seemed to have.

    I would close my eyes and witness darkness that never seemed to pass. You see, we tend to live within the past, even though it hurts to always finish last. We can never be first, can we? We're stuck inside of yesterday, as we play the same mistakes. I kept thinking, and I kept thinking until I overthought. Will these demons ever stop their screaming? Could I have changed the outcome if everything was different? It's a problem, isn't it? We feel the pain of loss but extend it to the loss of self. We portray these mixed feelings as if we're made to filter out tomorrow and stay within the moments that filled our heads with sorrow. It isn't easy when it comes to breaking. You somehow reach your limit and the void is all you see. It tempts you to come a little closer, as you're pulled in just by its exposure.

What does it mean to fall? You drastically begin to see the changes in your perception as you're drawn to anger. Your self-esteem begins to falter, and you feel the eyes stare into your soul, but they never seem to see you. They judge every little detail until you're crying on the floor and you lose your self-control. We find it hard to be individuals, so we try to put our faith into other people. We're scared of losing colour. We're scared to be blinded by our failure. The worst is all we seem to focus on when it comes to broken love. If only we could be stronger than we are, then none of it would matter. We'd forget about the person we once were and start to grow again, but the truth is right in front of us. We already grew until we supposedly met 'the one'. It isn't complicated, is it?

I used to believe that everyone was against me, because they would tell me to move on. I never understood the concept until it finally clicked inside my head. There's nothing to move on from. We pass through many faces in our lives. Some of them are here to stay, while others go their separate ways. We only attach ourselves to happiness, because we're scared to see the world in its entirety. I never knew this void would be a part of me. I never knew I was the only constant in my story. I was powerless when it came to love. It had me in its palm and held on as tight as it would want. I had to learn to be myself again, and that was the hardest part. You forget how to be alone again. You think of

Broken Pages

yourself as a tragedy without an end, but that's the beauty of being broken. You can feel it in your veins as your livelihood is recreated. You begin to change for the better, and the darkness becomes a friend.

I wanted to fix everything around me, but I was tired of pretence. I was tired of staring at these scars while underneath the stars. I had to learn to be myself, and here we are. I was never able to be happy, but now I bask in brokenness. I'm finally at peace with everything I think and feel. It was all I ever wanted. I had to find escape through the thoughts that I was hiding. It's never easy to admit you have a problem, but when you do, you realise you can use your flaws as an advantage. You may feel as though you have nothing left, but the truth is that you're limitless. You can do anything you want if you put your mind to it. We live to die, and we die to live. The secret is learning to adapt to what you're given. Never forget that every void is precious, even if it hurts.

Pedestal

We hurt each other. It's what we do. I don't think that others understand the way I felt for you. You were an angel without its wings, and I found you to be amazing. I was lost within your broken smile and your stunning eyes. Oh god, your eyes. They were the epitome of sincerity. I couldn't stop myself from falling. It was pretty hard to do when I was infected by this dream of you. The reason why I wanted to be with you is to feel less guilty. I wanted to tell the world you're mine and try to make you happy. I just wanted someone beside me in this fucked up life. I wanted to be the person that you could trust, and I've never shown you anything less than honesty. You deserve more than what you have, and to be honest, that's probably me.

I thought you're beautifully designed, except for how you treated me. I was yearning to find connection within this empty space between us, and I thought that you could save me. You were somehow the only person I could see when my walls were slowly caving. I hope you one day look back at what we never had. I hope you realise that I thought of you as someone I could love. That's how it was. I put you on a pedestal, and I felt like you were worth it, but now I live within reality. I was chasing dreams of being happy. I hope you felt it too, because I swear to God that I could love you. I'll repeat it once again. I knew that I could love you.

Face without a name

This is how it ends. This is my heart on a plate for you to see. I know it isn't easy to say that we failed, but sometimes people drift apart. I just wish that it didn't happen to us. These are the words I need to tell you before I break your heart. It isn't my decision, but something tells me that we're not made to be. We used to feel whole, but now it's time for our story to unfold. Whenever I'm with you, I feel like I'm alone. It's as if these moments that we cherished have somehow been erased. I can't see you the way I used to. Believe me, I try to, but the person that I used to love is somehow gone. I guess time is a killer, and it eventually killed us off. I know it doesn't make sense to be writing all these lines, but I need to empty out my head. This is my goodbye.

When we met, I could hardly think at all. I was going through the same old problems that I knew too well. I needed love to save me from this everlasting loneliness, but sadly, I broke us in the process. I was too far gone to keep our love alive. I held on for the sake of being happy, but there was no happiness left for me to see. I hope you understand that this is the only way for me to grow. I never meant to hurt you, but I fell in love with a lie. It's hard for me to even say this, but you were the only one who gave me hope. You were the brightest star within my universe, but your light had slowly faded, and you turned into a grievance. Before I even knew you, I was struggling to be happy, but in our cold embrace, my soul attached to yours, and everything seemed like it was worth it. You were the better part of me when the world was nothing more than tragic. I guess that's how we lost the magic. We were worlds apart and both of us imperfect. You were a star within the skies that never seemed to fly. You were flawed beyond design yet had so much heart behind your eyes. If I could hold you one more time, I would, but for my own peace of mind, I have to let you go. I have to say goodbye to everything I know. I hope that our paths will cross again, but for now; you'll be another face without a name.

Romance is dead

Romance is dead. This is what you want from me, isn't it? You want me to tell you about the end. I'm a firm believer of soulmates. That's what many people fail to understand. There are many souls roaming around the world, and we're attracted to their energy. We're hopelessly in love with the idea of being loved. I've said it once before, and I'll say it once again; your love will end in hurt. The truth is that we put too much importance on our past regrets, and romance is something we suddenly forget. We all long to be adored. We want instant gratification at the expense of dismissing what it means to be forever. We're humans. We're worse than animals when it comes to our decisions. Your heart may be searching for the one, but your mind disallows you from staying true together. It's the sad reality of being a romantic. You always want attention, but falter when it comes to what you need within the future.

Romance is dead because we killed it. We refused to keep the passion alive within our hearts, and the fire burnt away with its ashes scattered and lost within the wind. The remnants of our love had flown into the sea, as we progressed into temporary beings. It's how it is when you fall in love. You want to be remembered, but you become somewhat of a disease. The thought of you is worse than sickness, and it's a problem when you find a lover scorned. Their idea of romance begins to fade. They paint the skies with tragedy, as their world is turned upside down within their misery. It's how it is when you feel as though you're wronged. You lose your self-respect and have no confidence that you'll ever find another place that you belong.

There are many types of romances in the world, but there are those that defy the ages. Sadly, we never feel like we deserve it. We never want to give ourselves away to anyone, or we find distractions that only drain our souls. We have a problem with developing relationships due to our lack of trust. Do we truly believe that someone out there could be ours? We mostly search for lust. It's something that's been going on for a little bit too long. We put importance on appearance, yet never speak to each other's souls. We truly are afraid of being open. We're scared of vulnerability, and it prevents us from attaching ourselves romantically. We avoid the pain of loss by falling for the lies. You see the ones around you that you thought would be your happy ending? They're the ones who waste your time, and you know it deep inside. You're afraid to stop the cycle. You'll never find someone who feeds your soul if you remain within your circle. It's normal to have a fear of falling, especially when you fall in love.

The way we perceive these romantic dreams is somewhat of a tragedy. We want to control every single feeling, not knowing that we're slaves to the hearts we've been concealing. We never want to listen to the pounding. We never want to accept the rhythm is astounding. Have you ever felt connected? You stare into each other's eyes and the weight feels like it's been lifted. You feel at peace when you're lost inside a world that you've created. It isn't like interactions you've had before, because every sense is heightened. You feel their breath against your skin and your eyes have finally been opened. You want nothing more than to extend your time together and bask within their presence. It's part of romance that many of us will see within our lifetime yet avoid in case our dignity is broken.

We are the quiet ones. We quietly wait for love, as our minds are torn apart. We believe that waiting will achieve our longing to be loved. The problem with romance is that we never truly seek it. We search for vanity instead. We want to feel validation rather than respect. The two are quite different when it comes to our decisions. We want to surround ourselves with lovers in quantity, but quality is seemingly neglected. The truth is that you're the one to blame. You never let the right ones in, because you want to satisfy your need of being happy. This isn't a knock on the way you live, but if you feel as though you deserve more, you have to move away from what you know. It's the saddest part about relationships. We remain inside our choices. We want someone familiar, so we find the same shit we left behind. You have to be connected to remotely feel a certain way. We lie to one another to make our disparities okay. We want romance in an age where most of us are conditioned to want more of the same.

We live in a world where no one is connected. It may feel as though you are, but you wouldn't be reading this if you ever felt it. I've always been attracted to being broken, and once I realised romance is dead, I had to accept it. I had to push aside these feelings that made me feel inadequate. I was hopelessly addicted to the taste of red until I saw the world in blue. I observed everyone around me and saw infidelity. I thought humanity was better than what my eyes were seeing, but it was the same old story that kept repeating. What do you do when you find yourself in disagreement? I would see these happy faces, but none of them were perfect. They covered up the truth about how their love had slowly disconnected. It was sad. It truly was. I finally saw the insincerity that everyone was hiding and found that none of us are saints when it comes to romance or love in general.

We always want to find more than what we have, yet we stay within our boundaries as we fill our heads with doubt. We may be connected in some way, but romantically, we fail. We have this constant hope for revival, but when it's dead, there's no reason to provoke it. We choose the wrong people in our search for happiness. We always seem to do it. I used to wish that I could find someone that would guide me through this fucked up life we have. I wanted to stop my heart from bleeding, and I thought I should put my trust into broken beings. That's the problem that most of us have. We all have types. I'm attracted to those who hurt, because I find them to be fascinating. It's one of the reasons why I refuse to get close to people. I see them through their masks, and it somehow draws me in. I promised myself that I would never get close again. I know that romance ends in hurt, and I refuse to play the game.

I dream about tomorrow and everything between. I dream about the future and a broken queen. Sadly, it's only just a dream. You see, we all crave to find that special person, but the truth is that romance is imperfect. You feel the energy collide between your eyes and suddenly you've become infected. You want them in your life more than you can say. You think of them relentlessly, but those feelings go away. You're destined to be together for a short amount of time, because you never dare to see life with someone who may be your perfect fit. All of us will do it. We can be in a crowd of people and be clueless as to who is the one that'll make us feel like we're ready to push further. The truth is that we only use each other. We want to be whole so badly, that we'll somehow fall together, even if the face within the crowd is not meant to be our saviour.

I never knew the impact that love would have on me. You never do when it comes to emotional attachment. You want someone to see a different side of you; a side that no one else could ever view. We write these stories in our minds of

Broken Pages

what we hope romance will turn into but fail to realise that the end is a chapter we never put on paper. It's non-existent when we're desperate to find connection. The problem is that we never allow ourselves to find it. We have this emptiness that's deep inside us, and it claws away at everything that we believe in. We have these dreams that we'll find the perfect person, but the truth is that all of us are broken. It's in our nature to be cautious, because we're afraid of being open. It's hard to trust when the world is never as it seems. We place our souls in the hands of wolves and wonder why we suddenly get gnawed.

I've always wanted honesty, but honestly, I'm not an honest person. I used to be obsessed with love because of the way it made me question my existence. I was intrigued by the thought of giving myself away, because the reward was worth the risk. You may hurt from time to time, but these memories persist. It's what life is all about. You find a perfect match and waste each other's time until you say goodbye. The problem is that romance is an occurrence we may never experience until the end, because of how we were made to be. We'd rather chase the unattainable than find someone who truly does complete us. I wanted to believe that love is alive and well, but for now, I'll repeat it in my head until I believe these words I've said; romance is dead.

Heal together

Memories are all we ever have when we lose one another, because it never feels right to linger. It hurts to even be close to each other, so we leave in hopes of getting better. We're put in a position where we fall too deeply, too soon. We're almost as empty as a crescent moon. We've lost the better half of us, yet never understand the reason why it feels so dark. I wanted to chase after this idea of what it meant to be beside you. I wanted our love to somehow grow into peace for us, but our hearts had gone a little sideways, and neither of us could bear it. We were moving in directions out of our control, and in this silence, I thought you'd give me hope. I thought you'd be the glue that put me back together. I was so set on loving you, but I never had the chance to. I wonder why our story ended so abruptly, but maybe that's because I'm scared of being lonely.

You see, I was made to think too much, but sometimes it never feels like I thought enough. It's love. It's always love. You find a way out of your shell and hope to find someone to build upon these stories that you tell. I wanted to be part of a fairy tale, but I guess it became a little too grim to even sell. I believed in happiness and love for a little while, but as time went by, I had to learn to say goodbye. I had to put aside my dreams and break my fragile heart. It was the best decision I could think of when it came to a broken love. Nothing is made to be easy. Nothing is made to be seen as worthwhile, because eventually you'll start to lose your smile, like I did. You'll feel like you're neglected and somehow left behind. It's the sad reality of being bright, beautiful, and blind.

We have this constant need to create memories. We want to tell our children stories, but sometimes we never get to hold them. We never get to have what could have been, because we lost what used to be. It happens. It's a reason why we fail to understand ourselves. We regret too much, too soon when it comes to the bitter truth. It's something we do within our times of sadness, but dwelling is never progress. We could endlessly keep falling but never reach the bottom. That's what I love and hate about connection. You find yourself immersed in all its bliss, but the pain is hiding underneath the surface. We want the best outcome in every situation, not realising failure is part of every voyage. I managed to get hurt, but never thought that I would heal. I never knew the damage was repairable. I never knew being broken would be so beautiful.

You see, we're complicated beings. We feel too much, too soon. We're riddled with emotions that never last in their entirety. I had to remember what it was like to be alone. I was on this search for a better tomorrow. I wanted to let go. I wanted to magically feel whole again. It was part of a chapter that I never thought I'd live to tell. I was looking for answers in the midst of heartbreak, as I sought to find myself without

Broken Pages

a sense of love. It's what happens when you lose. You feel every part of your history come back to haunt you, as you feel lonelier than usual. You're made to fall so rigidly across the edges of your sanity. Your mind is something that goes first when it comes to the death of love and the start of loneliness. You never feel quite right when you're descending down towards the end. The truth is that you only end that chapter as you go on to the next. It may not be a swift transition, but I promise, you'll somehow find yourself again.

I'm not a bad person. Neither are you. Well, I hope we're not. We wonder why we're thrown the shortest end of the stick, but that's life. We're destined to fall apart but fix ourselves eventually. I had a problem of being self-aware and full of thoughts that led me to despair. I kept thinking, and I kept thinking until I drowned in tragedy. I never let it stop me, because I had to find my way back towards my story. I didn't think that anything would end the way it did before, because nothing truly stops the world. We may feel as though we're crashing but we never do. We move on, and this much I know is true. I'm glad we're sharing this moment together. I'm glad I can make you smile without even being there. I guess we're somehow connected somewhere within our distance. You found me as you battled through the storm, and you should be proud of that.

I may have wanted us to hurt together, but what is hurt without healing? I thought you had to find a lover to be able to save yourself in this fucked up world we live in, but maybe I was drawn to playing the victim. We're no different, I guess. We find it hard to digest, but parts of us are somehow connected. You may be wondering what I mean, but if you open up your eyes, you'll realise that I'm speaking to your soul, the way I always seem to do. That's the problem that I have. I used to be worried about being there for people too much. It's part of me that I always try to hide. I never thought about saving myself, because I was too focused on other people's lives. I don't label myself as selfless, because I'm not. I just want to share my pain with you, so hopefully we can heal together, as strangers seem to do in their endeavours.

It isn't easy being open. I never knew how hard I'd fall and how many times I'd cry. I had this need to find connection, but all I ever did was cause destruction. It was part of my recovery. I just wish I had a hand to hold through the darkness and in the cold. We never quite realise how alone we are until we stare up at the stars. They're so beautiful yet crowded in mystery and light. The problem is that we're unsure if they feel the same as us. We usually feel worse when we're in a crowd of people. It's natural. We see the smiles around us, as we try our best not to stare anyone in the eyes. It's part of humanity that I'll never understand. We're never comfortable when it comes to strangers, yet here I am, giving my heart on a plate for you to feast on. Maybe I'll feel less lonely, knowing you're feeling these words with me, although in a different time and place.

Broken Pages

The truth is that I've tried so hard not to cry while writing all these lines. You may be wondering where the poetry is right now, but this is more to me than creating rhymes. This is me in my entirety. This is me after heartbreak and loss. I'm a broken shade of beautiful, just like you, him, and her. I never found happiness after all of this. I never saw the world the same as other people. It's what happens when you crawl out of your lowest, and somehow make it up towards the surface. I never cared for being happy, because it never wanted me. I stopped chasing it after I found out it was damaging. I don't regret it, because now I'm finally at peace. I had some time to think, and when I think, I don't stop. It's a recurring theme with me. I just want to feel less lonely, as I guide you on this journey where we connect and heal together.

It's beautiful, isn't it? How these words convey a tragedy beyond what my lips could ever say. I've searched everywhere across the universe to capture what it is I'm missing, and it led me here to you. I want you to close your eyes for every word that you read next. This is me, the broken mess. I want to be your saviour so fucking badly, even if it hurts. I'm sorry if you feel these words too deeply. I've always felt for you. I truly have. You and I are cut from the same cloth. We bleed in blue with broken hearts. You're the reason why we're here, and I want you to know that this has always been for you.

Inept

There's this never-ending guilt that feeds off all our fears, yet through the pain we're here, lurking on the edge. There have been times where I've flirted with the notion of death, but I was never able to take a leap off of the ledge. I was scared of losing chances that I somehow thought I'd never get. The problem was never me to begin with; it was all the thoughts that crept into my head. I thought, and I thought until these tears were shed. The tragedy of falling deep into the blue is that you always feel inept. You breathe a little more than usual, as you try to catch your breath. The air around you tightens up your chest, and you're somehow left calming down your nerves. You wish for nothing but the best, but all you truly want is for someone else to notice. You want them to feel a glimpse of however much you hurt. But they don't. You're alone.

You try to fight the empty spaces that leave you restless, but it's too much to come to terms with. You're running out of time, but the clock is slowly ticking. It's as if the world is slipping through your fingers and the dark is covering all the light around you. You're susceptible to pain, so you down another bottle. You want to erase the worries that you have with something tangible. The problem with feeling like you're falling is that no one else can see you, or so it feels. You shut out everyone who's there, because you're scared. You'd

Broken Pages

rather lose people than be seen as fragile. You see, we hold a thousand scars that never seem to heal. We lock them up inside until we lose our value.

I'm attracted to the pain of life. Isn't it weird how most of us are? We look for distractions to save us from falling into the fire. It's how we cope with transitional desires. We always assume that everything will remain unchanged, failing to see through what's far from the same. I want to be real with you. I want to show you all my scars. I was once afraid to fly because I was scared to crash into the stars. We always want perfection in a world where everything feels so fucking distant. We try to grab the sun, not knowing it'll burn us. We're confusingly atrocious, or that's how it feels when we're walking around without a purpose. We're simple beings lost in this plane we call existence, and I wish that some of us could see it. We fall madly in love with the idea of being connected yet we're too blind to see underneath the surface. It's as if we somehow lose our senses.

The moments that we cherish slowly fade into the distance. We find a picture from a year ago and our happiness begins to perish. It's as if these memories were made to kill us, as the silence seeps into our souls with no admittance. This feeling that we have is pretty mutual. We find escape within reality to hurt a little less, as our eyes tilt away from pages that were left behind in history. It may not make any sense now, but in the future, you'll understand me. We were born to make mistakes, and even in the cold, it feels as though we're drowning. We have this constant reminder that we'll never cross the boundaries, yet we never ask the question of who made these rules we follow. That's the beautiful thing about the unknown. We're always unsure about tomorrow and what it brings, but we still limit ourselves to the way we overthink. It's deemed to be a problem because sometimes people sink. They fail to understand it as much as they had hoped and suddenly it's tainted with the same rhetoric.

The secret to overthinking? It's being aware of all your thoughts and surroundings. You have to let yourself go completely to find yourself again. You have to see from every point of view to understand reality from fiction. We think, and we think until we overthink. What is the problem? What is the solution? Why do we feel inadequate? We always fall victim to the haze. It's what happens when we trust our thoughts a little too much. We believe in everything that's floating in our heads until we convincingly have nothing left. We're our own worst enemies, especially when we go from one thought to the next.

The same lines repeated are the ones that hit the hardest, and as you can see, I'm the broken artist. I thought about the promises that were made to break and how I was afflicted. I wanted nothing more than to breathe within this space that felt constricted. My mind was flooded without reason, as I hurt myself with words I never spoke of. We're destructive when it comes to overthinking, and I seemed to be no different. I was on the edge for many years, yet always felt as though I'm stuck far off in the distance. The screams were shattering everything that I believed in as my sanity was broken. You flirt with the idea of death for so long that you become accustomed. It doesn't faze you after a while, because you've somehow died a thousand times over in your mind. I know the struggle of being. I've felt my bones stiffen at the thought of leaving, but what I'd leave behind is a heart that never stopped its bleeding. I went from red to blue in seconds, as I questioned this tragic life I'm leading.

We build our walls to break, but most of us fear what's underneath. The remedy to death is always life. You may feel as though you're gasping for air, but all of it is self-inflicted. You put yourself in a position where you're made to feel like you're the victim. I've tasted the bitterness of seclusion and the power of redemption. I wanted to move past the hate that I was given, and in the process, I crumbled into pieces. I always wanted the world to be my oyster, but I hated the expression. I had this constant need for more, but I was always afraid of being in control. I never thought I could be. It's how I was when I had a fear of being broken. I disallowed myself to open my eyes in my time of dying, and I was dying for salvation.

We never realise what's in store for us until we allow our minds to be open. We're hopelessly searching for acceptance

Broken Pages

in a place where breathing is restricted. It's pretty sad to be human, but it's even worse to be afflicted. You dream about the universe, but you're stuck inside a maze. I never wanted it to happen, but it did. I was falsely led to nowhere, and somehow made it my home when I got there. That's the problem with what we do and how we feel. We think we're incapable of changing our reality, but when you finally see the truth, you move the world around you. We're so fucking connected. I keep saying it. I keep mouthing all these words as they appear before me. I just want to create a sense of beauty. I want to lift this void that I've been fighting. I've been lost and empty, but this is all of me. Right now. Right here. This is me in my entirety. These are the words that I need to tell you to somehow set you free.

You'll be led to believe in lies by many of the people around you. The truth is that human interaction is forced, because we want to feel as though we're real. We want to break apart the loneliness and shed light against our walls. I've been there. I've done that. I know how you feel in every single way possible. I'm addicted to the pain and I seem to love it. It's a sad truth in a life that I never really wanted. We're so feeble when it comes to other people. They drive us into the ground without a care, but all of us are alike. You may be the villain in someone else's life yet not realise the damage that you've done. We love to play the victim, don't we? I used to believe that the world was against me. I thought I could do no wrong, but I guess I was partly to blame for making others cry. I just do it sometimes. It happens. I can't control the anger. I'm not a perfect person. None of us are. We only hide the truths to build upon our lies. I was tired of thinking that I'm selfless, when reality was different.

I would always make myself the hero, but little did I know that I was pretty much an asshole. It's that kind of self-awareness that brings it all together. I saw everyone around me trying to be the better person, but all of them were inadequately equipped to be the voice of reason. We're flawed as fuck, and my flaws aren't worth giving up. They make me human. They give me a reason to keep on going. I wouldn't be able to fight the battles that I've faced if I removed the ugliness of life. It's a strength that many find a weakness, but here I am, yet again, the broken artist. I breathe light into the darkness, but never forget that I'm infected by this illness. I'm an overthinker without boundaries and I see the depth within humanity. I had this strong desire to let go of insecurity, but my heart was bleeding blue in all of its humility.

We never see ourselves for who we are. We always show people what we want them to see, and that's a conflict of self. We want to erase the dreams we once held to have a bit of normalcy. We lose our trust because no one ever feels enough. Believe me, I know how draining it is to be out of touch. We claw our way into people's hearts, expecting a bit of decency, but all they do is break our trust. They want to have control over us, because we give too much and expect a little less. We used to want more but life had changed our way of thinking. We never feel like we deserve it. Maybe because we feel a little bit inept. It's a beautiful word yet so full of regret. You put your effort into being happy but change never comes into effect. You slowly move downwards as the pain forces you to sink. It's what most of us will do when we have trouble finding solid ground. We try to put the brokenness aside as we fall without a sound. It's how we face the truth when all we do is lie.

The problem is always in front of us. I always wanted to dream more than I would live. I ran through these crowded faces, belittling everything that I believed in. I never knew that I was breaking. I gave too much for little in return. It's part of being human, I guess. We expect to be given the same amount of respect, but sometimes it's something that we never get. We're unappreciated and undervalued yet we always try our best to see the journey though. We're fragile pieces of art, lost within a portrait we call life. It's a tough pill to swallow, but behind your eyes is someone who breaks apart at nightfall. You think about your past regrets, because underneath the stars, you seem to be more thoughtful.

The darkest days will come, but when they do, they're quickly gone. We refuse to see that side of life, because we hate to see everything as temporary. We're unfortunately inept, aren't we? A moment of hurt should never last a lifetime, yet none of us ever feel like that's the truth. We linger on the saddest stories that shaped us into who we are today, but will it be who we are tomorrow? Everything is uncertain, yet all we do is stop ourselves from living. We let our pasts define us when the future hasn't even started. No matter how you feel, no matter what you do, you'll always be afraid of stepping out into the world. I never allowed myself any room for growth. I attached myself to ideas that only made me worse. I was living without a sense of purpose, and it clearly seemed to show. I was tired of being who I was before, and I had to let these feelings go.

I always thought I was incapable of smiling. I always thought I was unable to be real. The perception that I left myself with was nothing close to what I wanted. We place ourselves lower than everybody else. Maybe because we lack self-love, or we love to hold self-pity. The truth is always simple, yet we somehow enjoy complexity. We want to question everything, not because we're empty, but because we hurt ourselves to feel. You don't deserve to cry over what your mind is telling you. You're more than capable of finding whatever it is you're searching for. You're human and you're flawed, but life is made of moments that somehow make you whole. We may be numb from time to time but it's part of the unknown. It's the only way for us to grow.

The catalyst

There are words that we hide, because being expressive is a curse. We're unsure of who to trust, as we conceal who we truly are. We're tired of rejection. We're tired of losing friends. It's a sad reality we live in, and it's worse because we share each other's burdens. We're all connected in some way, and it's sad to see us detach ourselves whenever we're afraid. It's part of humanity that irks most of us each day. We know that we co-exist but fail to draw the line where most of us will fit. It's how we disconnect that truly is surprising. We wish to hide ourselves behind white lies and happy faces. It's the way we seem to be when our smiles are slowly fading.

We're never satisfied when it comes to life. We feel like we deserve more than what we have. It's as if we're driven by greed, but shy away from danger. We're mostly scared to push a little further. We want to feel affection, but success is put aside, because it's perceived to be too far out of our reach. The dreams that keep us sleeping are the ones we miss the most. We want them to be lucid, so we can have control. We dream of happiness yet have zero sight of it. Does it truly exist, or do we put ourselves at risk? We're influenced into wanting pretty things, but never ask ourselves how they could possibly benefit the future. We base our assumptions on the words of others, because we're moulded by society and all of its discoveries. We wonder how it would be if we were living in someone else's skin. It's sad, it truly is.

We place importance on our appearance. It's how it's always been. We want the perfect body, yet never try to achieve the perfect mind. The truth is nothing can be perfect, not even all these words that I've been crafting. I used to want perfection, but suddenly I realised that mistakes were all I made. They shaped me into who I am today. I would look around and see different shades of beautiful, and I found myself to be a broken angel. I was never made to be a perfect soul, and I could see it clearly as I fell down each and every hole. The strength I had to crawl was what made me appreciate the world.

It's beautiful, isn't it? I can have a conversation in my head and portray it in these words. I know you understand me. We're connected. So fucking connected, yet none of us can see it. We feel the same emotions, and we breathe the same air, but why do we feel like none of this is real? We blankly stare at walls, as we try not to lose ourselves. We keep thinking, and we keep thinking until we overthink. That's the reason why we never sink. We put our thoughts in everything we do. We want nothing more than to get through, as each day brings us something new. The saddest part is that our mind is a catalyst that few of us ever seem to get. We form beliefs and attitudes that lead us to places of regret, as we long to be accepted. Acceptance. What a fucking word that fills us up with guilt.

We wish to be accepted into circles that never do us good, yet we fight for something better, wishing that they would. The truth is devaluing yourself for others should never be a virtue. Putting trust in other people will ultimately hurt you. I'm sorry, but it's true. We somehow distance ourselves to create space, but in doing so, we lose friends we thought would never be erased. We live our individual lives and have no room for anybody else. It's a truth that no one ever tells you. I wanted to disappear, because all I saw was red, but I had some time to think and found myself instead.

There's a problem that we have with overthinking. We're threatened by the thoughts, as they overwhelm us in their flocks. It's something out of our control, but it opens up our eyes to truths that were obstructed from our view. There are moments where we feel too much, and our minds seem to fuck us up. It's humanity at its worst, or so it feels. We want to take away the pain but heighten it instead. The journey of an overthinker is one which prides itself on hurt. We burn ourselves a thousand times until we push aside regret. I struggled with acceptance, but I found the courage to let go. I accepted the world as what it is, and now nothing seems to hurt me anymore, because I finally fought and won the war.

Behind this skin

You hurt. I know you do. You're human, and I am too. That's the beautiful thing about humanity. We fall and we rise. We hurt and we heal. There is no limit to whatever it is that we feel. The saddest part of humanity is what it means to be real. We feel the ache of life and death, as we dream of better days. You feel alone, I know you do. It's a problem that many of us have, as we walk into the cold. We want to grab attention, but it's too heavy for us to hold. We value admiration more than what is told. We crave to be seen behind the curtain that hides our troubled souls. However, it's quite the task to be vulnerable enough to let others know our pain.

When you fall, you fall hard. You fall into every part of yesterday, as you're plunged into the past. You recreate these memories that truly never last. You want to make amends for what you've done and try to be forgiven for everything that's wrong. The words you want to say are slightly altered, because you're afraid of making more mistakes. You're a fallen angel, because inside, you're absolutely beautiful. We hurt ourselves before every stage that comes. We somehow push these thoughts towards negatives when positivity is hard for us to find. It's how we deal with change, or better yet, how we avoid the inevitable to be able to stay the same. It isn't a productive way to be, but we fear that our grief will suddenly increase. I've been living in fear of happiness for as long as I can remember. It's the only path that drew me into closure. I wanted to know the reasons why I hurt and why I felt so hopeless. I was full of flaws and insecurities, and I still am in my entirety.

I wanted to connect to everyone. I craved it like an addict. I wanted to show people that life is more than what it is. That's the problem we all have. We take life for granted. We feel alienated, as we put ourselves at risk of overthinking, but our walls never break completely. We feel as though we're empty, when in reality we feel a thousand emotions all at once. I used to believe that I was going nowhere, and I tried my best to somehow get there. I would create worlds inside my head to escape from a reality that felt so non-existent. I'm an overthinker, it's what I do best. The truth is that I was scared of what it means to live. I was scared of being happy, because I couldn't see the benefits. Behind this skin is someone who hurts within. That's what I used to tell myself every single day. I was struggling with connection. I was struggling to even breathe. My worries increased without a warning, as these thoughts of disappearing emerged without a reason. I couldn't promise that I'll see tomorrow, because I lived in yesterday and all its sorrow.

We're complicated beings. We have a need to smile when the world is truly fucked. Does it mean we're selfish or do we practice this term called self-love? All of it is bullshit. We tell each other lies, because we want to sell happiness in our darkest times. I always avoided false hope, because I truly felt alone. I accepted the fate that I was given and made the most of it. Behind the skin you live in is someone who hurts within.

Broken Pages

I've felt it. I still do. There's no magical way to fix it. That's the problem with avoidance. You become cynical about the world around you. You crave for acceptance in an otherwise sad situation. You feel like you could be better, but you don't realise that you're pulling yourself down further.

There will always be a longing deep inside you that never lets you sleep. I've faced it all before. I was living in the skin of someone who hurts within. I expected more from life than this, but I let myself be wasted. I fell into depression and tried to keep my head above the water. I wanted to find happiness. I truly did. I was aimlessly searching for it in places that I shouldn't. I would give my time to people that would only turn to strangers. I had nothing left to feel, as I suppressed myself for the benefit of living. I was selfishly trying to change myself. I guess that's the reason why I hurt the most. I never wanted to be me, because I was never happy.

There's too much emphasis on leading happy lives, and it seems to bring us down. We see what others have and wonder why we're so detached. We become jealous of emotions too deeply, yet so quickly. We base our value on those around us, yet never feel as though we're individuals. I never wanted to be an imitation. I had to appreciate what I was given yet be cursed with overthinking. I was obsessed with repeating the past I knew too well. I would go through all these words and faces, but now they've turned to nothing. The truth is that I had to choose to be broken, so I could safely say that behind this skin is someone who found the will to win.

Wasting breath on you

I'm drawn to your beautiful smile, knowing that everything will suddenly fall apart around us. That's how it is when it comes to attraction. We breathe each other in like oxygen, but then we gasp for air when we near the end. We become detached too quickly, as we shift our focus back to loneliness. The truth has always been hard to handle. You find someone who completes you, but the story remains the same. You're too young or old to fall in love, or at least that's what your mind will tell you. There never is an in between. You break at the thought of being lonely, because you fail to live within reality. I just wish that I could tell you the way I felt more poetically. These words are formed from memories, and even if you never saw me the way I saw you, I still remember the reasons why I was attracted to everything you do.

I never gave you anything less than honesty, and honestly, I was too honest to save you from the darkness. I always felt like you were perfect, and I somehow tricked myself into believing you were more important than the love I lost. That's the saddest truth that I'm willing to admit. I wanted to light these skies with a broken shade of blue. I was ready to give my heart to you. It's a sad situation when you think about it. I was endlessly trying to be yours, yet I could never find the words to illustrate the way I felt. There was no one else that caught my eye the way you did. I was lost in every thought and word you ever said. I was quickly connected to something that was never even there, as I battled through a one-sided love affair.

You see, people like you are hard to come by. You seem to be the crutch that holds everything together. I wanted you to be what I could never be. I wanted you to be my saviour. You distracted me from thinking, but sadly, I was on a path that led me nowhere, yet I was glad that you were there. I became accustomed to your presence and it made me feel less lonely. It's all I ever wanted. I just needed someone to stop me from running to the edge. I'm sorry it had to be you, but it happens. We put our affection where it isn't wanted. We place our faith in people who give us hope that we'll survive until tomorrow. You were the brightest part of my day, even though I knew you would one day go away. I built a sad situation in my head and it only made me worse. It's what I do to make it hurt a little less. I wish you knew the strength you gave me. I wouldn't be here if it weren't for you.

There were many times where I would stare at you and drift into my thoughts. I would think about the creases in your eyes every time you'd try to hide your smile. You were like forbidden fruit, and sure enough, you had me addicted to the taste. You were genuinely beautiful in each and every way, or so I felt. We're blinded by the truth. We always create perceptions in our heads that differ from what's real. I replaced the negatives to keep myself content. I had to. I

Broken Pages

erased your insecurities to build you up into something that you weren't. It was a sad situation that somehow left me burnt. I never wanted it to be like this, but life is sometimes cruel. I was falling head over heels without listening to truths. I had this idea of us that stuck to me like glue, and I was almost ready to be in love with you. But these stories never work to my advantage, and it's the reason why people leave me, because I'm never less than honest.

I had a fixation with wanting to save you. It's what broken people do. They give all they have to give to make others feel better within this world of solitude. I wanted to be your saviour. I needed to shield you from the harm surrounding you. It isn't easy being like this, but I could say the same for you. You never knew the truth. You never wanted to. There's always something we miss when it comes to passion. We never assess the outcomes that are bound to happen. The problem was that I had a thousand conversations with you inside my head yet all of them somehow led to silence. I felt you slipping through my fingers as I dreamt about the end. I knew goodbye was coming. I knew the quiet storm would one day fade before me. I could tell you I was ready, but no one's ever ready to feel detached from what used to be.

I felt this fire burning as I watched us grow apart. I filled my head with worry when I couldn't heal this broken heart. You threw me into places I didn't want to go to. I once

Broken Pages

thought you were the breath of air I needed during my collapse. I felt alive within your presence, but sadly, the situation was never in our favour. We were two souls without a home, and I guess we never did deserve it. The time we spent together was built on lies that kept on bleeding. The clock was slowly ticking as I lost touch of what it was that I was seeing. I saw you for more than what you're worth, and that's the truth I seem to tell myself. The saddest situations are those that break us without a reason, and now I see things clearly, I was only wasting breath on you.

The victim

Who am I designed to be? I look at the world as if I've lost my sanity. I'm affected by the worst of humanity, and it makes me sick to feel as though I'm lonely. I'm the victim. The one who needs someone to save them. I always allow myself to be taken advantage of, but sometimes, I find it hard to resurface. I'm lost. I'm afraid. I'm alone. The same three words keep repeating, as I try to smile with the possibility of breaking. It's confusing, to say the least.

I've felt alone in the company of others, and I'm lost within this loneliness. I have a fear of being used, but to be honest, I've never been one to tell the truth. I just wish that I could wake up from this nightmare and safely say I'm letting go of how I feel. I'm always feeling if you haven't noticed. It's part of me that I wish never existed, but what can I do? I'm labelled as the victim in my own mind, but that's far from what is true.

The villain

I'm a tragedy. I'm a monster. I'm the reason someone cries. I guess it's part of being human. We put ourselves in places where we shouldn't. I'm the broken. I'm the villain. It's the reason why I'm numb. I played with fire until the better side of me was gone. I burnt down all these bridges to get a glimpse of ecstasy. I pushed away humanity to surrender all my sanity. I'm infectious. I'm indecisive. I'm constantly reminded of why I'm dangerous.

I'm the most toxic person you will ever meet, or so it seems. I guess it's how I present myself. I show the world a side of me that's disguised with emptiness. I'm a broken soul without a home. It's the reason why I feel alone. I guess it's the same story we all share; we feel alone when no one else is there. I used to plead to have connection, but no one heard my prayers. Maybe it's the reason why I'm meant to be the villain. No matter what I do, I feel as though I'm the one to blame. I just wish that someone could see behind my eyes, rather than label me as the villain they despise.

The saviour

I've always been attracted to vulnerability. I've always wanted to touch someone's heart and feel their pain. I want to be let in. I want to have the closeness that most of us desire. It's complicated how our brains are wired. We're set on love and its distractions. We want to avoid our own feelings by taking on another's. I long to be connected. I long to be in love. I want to see through the windows of a soul and look at everything that it beholds. I'm in love with the idea that I could be somebody's saviour, but it's hard to say, because I'm also in need of saving.

I keep falling under pressure of being this picture perfect person. It's hard for me to function when this weight is on my shoulders. I'm made to engage with others, as if they're attached to my aching heart. It's the reason why I break apart. Everybody's drawn to me for help, but who can I save if it's hard to save myself? I struggle with the pain of going nowhere, as I'm labelled as the saviour. I guess it's how the story goes when you're damaged goods. No one sees the truth except for the person in the mirror.

The witness

We forget that multiple views exist. I'm the witness. I've seen the victim fall apart too many times, as the villain makes them lose their smile. I rarely see a saviour worth a mention, but maybe I'm just blind. I always look away from conflict, because all I want is peace. I seem to get caught up even when I'm hiding from my peers. I'm the bystander that everyone approaches when the trouble's brewing. I never have contact until they look outside their circle. They only seem to flock to me whenever they have problems. I float around the crowd, yet none of them treat me like we're close. I guess I'm just a ghost.

I prefer to be alone, so I stay somewhere out of reach. I'd rather not choose between anyone at all. I've seen people come and go, but it still hurts, you know? They use me to feel like they were right. They never care about the person crying out inside. I'm the one that's left to their own devices, as I quietly wait for arguments to happen. The problem is that I'm too available to decline anyone's advances. I'm an easy target. I'm forgotten. I'm the witness, and I just wish I could feel like I wasn't worthless.

Friendship fades

We choose the people that we keep. You may have friends that are out of reach, but are they worth the loss of sleep? We attach ourselves to nothing, as we desperately crave to be adored. We want acceptance from those around us yet fall apart when they ultimately hurt us. There have been times where I've fallen for people's words. I had a lapse in judgement, and my thoughts decayed into resentment. I wondered why I was so trusting, and where would I be if situations never found me.

Everyone is temporary. Friendship fades as you grow apart from one another. It may sound pessimistic, but this is what it means to be a realist. It's something none of us will ever understand. No one is obligated to stay, but we assume that they'll never go away. We have this need to surround ourselves with people, because loneliness is hard for us to handle. We place them in these empty spaces to prevent ourselves from breaking. Our isolated thoughts begin to go away, because we create a false escape.

We numb the pain of feeling, but only for a second, or so it feels. There will come a time where you feel your friends are fading. It's a natural occurrence that may happen more than once within your lifetime. It doesn't mean that you've failed, it just means you grew apart. The reason we break down is because we're caught by surprise. We hold on to the past that we held so close and dearly, but we're only holding on to hope. The sad truth is that we were never made to be forever. You have to learn to let each other go. It isn't an easy task, but it's better than living in the past. We give too much in hopes of being happy. I guess it's hard to find acceptance when we desperately try to feel less lonely. It's always on our minds, isn't it? We have this fear of being left behind. We never want to admit it, but it's there. We put ourselves in places that we should never be in just to feel like we're still breathing. I always wanted to know if there's something wrong with me. Why do people leave? Am I the problem? It's how we try to make sense of what is real. We try to put the blame on ourselves so we can simply heal. It isn't your fault. It never is. We constantly change throughout the years until suddenly we're back to being strangers.

We never seem to understand the reasons why we faded. We used to have it all, the smiles and pretty faces. Nothing is ever ugly when it comes to friendship until we're faced with our eventual endings. The loss always strikes the hardest, as we search for answers as to why something so beautiful could end in hatred. We want everything to last for ages, unknowingly filling our heads with ideas that are less than perfect. It's the fear of being alone, isn't it? We find a place to fit in this fucked up universe, but sadly all our efforts are erased within a measly minute. It's saddening to say it, but friendship fades faster than the seasons change. We always want someone to be there, so we try to avoid the pain of being lonesome. It's the only way for us to feel as though we're human. We connect without a reason, but in our minds it's more than just distraction. You see, I keep thinking, and I keep thinking until I overthink. Do we truly belong forever? We put so much pressure on each other. None of us can ever truly be there. We have our own lives to live, and sometimes others rarely fit.

I saw the truth behind the lies of friendship. I let people use me for their own gain just to be a better person. I was allowing myself to be taken advantage of when I was breaking. I hated the feeling of being lonely. I just wanted something to give me a reason to stay grounded when I felt like I was falling. That's the problem that we have with letting others in; we somehow let ourselves become a victim. You meet strangers everywhere you go, and you wonder if any of them will be the one to give you more than hope. It's natural. We want to be noticed. We want someone to see us, but it's so hard when everything seems to turn out sour.

We believe in trusting people because life is too short, but then we fall into a trap of being ridiculed and left questioning our worth. Giving too much of yourself is unforgivable, or so it seems. You want the best outcome, even if it means to belittle yourself for the benefit of others. We go to great lengths to keep all of our friends, because life without them would hardly make sense, or will it? How many times can you trust someone until you feel alone? It's what we do to prevent people from leaving. We give them all our trust, in hopes that they'll see our worth to ultimately stay.

Nothing is as it seems when it comes to connection. It's what we fear and what we love. We learn to let our walls down for another individual, but then the walls decay and

Broken Pages

we're left dreaming of whatever used to be. We sporadically become undone, as we fight the pain of loss. We lose interest in one another too quickly when we roam the world around us. Our ideas begin to shift and somehow what we had before becomes a burden. It's how our stories unfold as the years begin to pass and the memories become more distant. We put a lot of thought into time and healing, and it's for good reason. We're never the same person that we were prior, and that's something most of us will fail to realise.

We want to keep everyone around us, even if they only seem to hurt us. We need to find some space to breathe, because we can't keep running from disaster. I know you fear the future. You're scared of being lonely without the friends that you hold dearly. It's life. We fill the empty chapters as we experience the world and what's in store for us. It's how these broken pages seem to ink themselves into existence. The hardest part about being stuck somewhere that only brings you down is that you fill your story with nothing more than hate, not realising that friendship was made to fade.

Damsel in distress

She was on the verge of leaving, as her eyes were pointed at the skies. I saw sadness fill her up, as I was staring blankly at her smile. Depression was among her and she felt the need to hide. I know it's hard to muster, but all she wanted was to belong somewhere other than her mind. She had a thousand doubts that cut her into pieces, yet she never seemed to present herself as broken. She could see the light beyond her eyes, as she gave up searching for resistance. This life that she created was nothing that she wanted, and her hope was non-existent. She was an overthinker, and her decisions only made her weaker. It felt like she was going nowhere, because the world is unforgiving. She was such a beautiful disaster. What a shame that she was sinking.

Her eyes told a story that no one cared to read. They carried a history of hatred, as she threw her soul away. She could barely see the future, and her ending was all that she would crave. She used to have the courage to speak her mind before this, but as the years went on, her innocence was taken. She trusted too much and fell a little harder. She was the pinnacle of cautiousness, and her fear of being loved is what made her feel emotionless. She was perfectly imperfect, or that's what she would say to soften her mistakes. The truth is that she was only human but never understood it. She lacked the need to love because she felt that it would hurt, that is until we met by chance and the chemistry was effortless.

You build each other up within your minds to a point where you're attached. I admired her more than you could imagine. She was courageous yet made to believe that she was limited. I wanted to read the story behind her eyes, but she never gave me room to explore the truths that she would hide. She had dreams of being found but nothing seemed to fuel her fire. She felt as though the only direction she was heading to was south. She crumbled at the sight of strangers, fearing for the worst. She seemed to always feel misplaced, even in the company of others. Her smile made it clear that she was struggling, not because it was forced, but because she wore it even when she cried.

I wanted to remove her silent screams, but I fell in love with her insecurities. She was someone that I would never change. That's the problem with our perceptions of love. We want to change each other for the better rather than accept the person that we're seeing. I found comfort within her tragedy, as I saw her for what no one else could see. There's a calming relief when being together without certainty. You somehow become attracted to whatever it is that could be. I was drawn to her instantly without any form of regret. I wanted to see her grow, even if it meant that my dignity would fade. She reserved herself without a reason. She was tired of trusting friends with mixed feelings. The truth is that she was hopeless. She had this need for love, but no one gave her what she desired. She wanted to be held through nights of terror, however, no one understood her.

I would always wonder where we're going and if we'll ever truly get there. She gave me a glimpse of who she was as she stood there in the cold, waiting for the rain. She loved the sense of adrenaline. She was chaos while I was solace. We were far apart yet closer than anyone could fathom. She was never human to me, because she was an angel, although emptier than usual. I could never understand what brought us here together. I was lost in every single moment, trying to secure a place within her future. It was never easy being with her. She had nothing left to lose and nothing left to gain. She never wanted me to be there to see her through the pain. Sometimes you have to realise that you should never save anyone from themselves. You have to give them space until eventually you've been erased. We always assume that every ending will steer into our favour, but reality is different. We're never able to be happy when we place the world on each other's shoulders.

She kept her distance, as if to tell me that it's over. She never needed anyone. Do you know how hard it is to belong when you feel like you're alone? It's saddening to say it, but I was afraid of what would be if I left her to be here without me. We're drawn together at the worst times, sometimes. She would whisper in my ear, as the morning light would suddenly appear. The hours felt like minutes whenever she was here. We attach ourselves to the belief that someone could be good for us but end up being disappointed when they break our trust. It's the wildest side of human nature that we seemingly avoid. I wanted to give her meaning, because I knew she was slowly fading. She was the missing piece in my universe for one, and loneliness was what we shared like a single bullet in a loaded gun.

We revealed secrets and regrets during quiet nights. We'd converse about the world and the harm that seemed to kill our souls. We were connected beyond actions and even words. We knew each other's pain because we felt alive within our shared embrace. Connection is a beautiful thing, isn't it? You mend the pieces of yourselves that never seemed to heal. You live for every moment, as you taste the bitterness of being. You rarely find it in this instance of reality, but when you do, it's nothing less than perfect. You're motivated to feel harder than you ever have before. You want to set everything on fire, as serendipity fills the void inside your soul. I was amazed to be able to feel more human. I felt like I belonged when the world was cold and distant. I guess that was the problem. Too much happiness can kill you, so you lose what you had and then some. Everyone will change at some point. You sense their energy has shifted, and you realise what you had was a memory that never stopped repeating.

Broken Pages

She was a dark horse in a race that never seemed to have a winner. She would take a step forward, but another two back. She never knew exactly what she wanted or what she had. The saddest truth is that everything was made to fade. I held her up in high regard, but she never did the same. She was disconnected more than I can say. She wanted love to be her calling. She wanted to find a way out of being lost inside this stressful whirlwind. I knew I had to give her patience, but I neglected my own happiness. We somehow seem to put importance on making others happy, disregarding what we feel inside. We want the best for them, even if it means ignoring what might be best for us. We depend on them so easily that we're afraid to give them up.

She would feed me lies to keep me satisfied. She had the need to hide, even when I knew the truth. It took some time to realise that everything was gone. It's hard to admit that you're staring at love's demise. You want to change reality into something good, but the truth is you never should. We always want to keep around the old rather than accept the new, so we hold on dearly to what we have, because we're scared of the unknown. The memories remain forever, but we refuse to understand that, so we force ourselves to forget. The problem with forgetting is that you remember every single detail, as your mind pushes you to trouble. You become surrounded by the past to a point where you'd rather live outside the moment, but you never live at all.

Broken Pages

There were so many unsaid words between us. It's how it is when you feel the need to love. It sounds absurd, but nothing has felt truer than trying to combine into one. I was feeding my addiction with her breath and energy. I wanted her to be close to me. She was a hazard and I was being careless. I wanted to be in love with the idea of happiness, but sometimes we're not meant to chase it. We become attracted to the future, to the pain. We want to reignite the flame we thought we lost. We're blinded by everything around us, as we give ourselves away. I really wish that she could see me, but I guess it's hard to see a fool. She was the greatest part of my existence for a short amount of time. She made the days brighter with her wicked smile, but the problem was that she was never mine.

I was lost within the moment. Nothing ever seems to work when you're stuck inside your head. You want to believe that you can hold the world, when in reality, you're just a broken shell. I thought she was my lifeline, but I was losing hope within her presence. She kept herself hidden so no one else could see her. She wanted nothing more than reassurance. She needed someone there to give her life a little meaning, but sadly, she never truly cared about me. I opened up my eyes, but the damage had been done. I promised myself not to be the one she could rely on. She was perceived to be the saviour, but to me she was the damsel in distress, and I was the broken king himself.

Gaslight

There was a history of abuse that put her into silence. She was panicking about the future, because she couldn't see anything that's good. She never understood why anyone would hurt her, but she was naïve enough to trust him. The cruellest moments are shared between those who give and those who take. She was an empty shade of broken that no one could explain. Her heart was sewn to his, yet he was never the hope that she had wanted.

He put her down without a thought, because he wanted to be controlling. He saw a side of her that no one could ever see, and he loved the idea that she was his. He was toxic to her health, mentally and physically. He made her fall for lies and gaslighted everything that she believed. Her sanity was questioned, as she was constantly in a state of thinking, trying to find a way to finally escape him. She wanted love to be her cure, but sadly, her story wasn't perfect. She had no courage to ever leave him. She thought the world would end, because she became dependent. He was her support, yet the reason why she fell.

The silence was almost deafening, as she felt his arms around her. She wanted to let go, but he kept her on his leash. No one ever knew the pain that she had felt. She would cry at night, wondering what tomorrow holds. She was so beautiful yet infected by the cold. She let him disregard her life completely, as her mind was torn to pieces. Her heart bled

Broken Pages

blue, just like me, and even you. She didn't know her worth and it was part of her distress. She was frantically searching for forgiveness, not realising that she never did deserve this. She was made to believe that reality is distorted. Her world was slowly gaslit, as he controlled her every thought with lies that made her distant.

She neglected everything around her while she slowly disconnected. She lost her will to fight, because she knew the world was made to be unkind. She was hoping that their love would revert to the way it was before. She never expected him to change, but as the years progressed, it was her voice that he repressed. He used to be ambitious and treat her the way that she deserves. He would whisper lies into her ear to make her believe that he would never leave. She was told that she was beautiful, as he picked apart her fragile soul. He manipulated her until she couldn't see herself without him in the future.

She was always wondering how he's feeling. She never wanted to displease him. She was stuck in a constant state of dreaming, and she made him the sole reason why she's breathing. She was clearly being mistreated, yet she couldn't even see it. He would break down her self-esteem, in hopes that she would forever be his queen. This isn't anything close to love and what it means, but there are wolves among us who tear into our skin and control the way we think. She finally began to question why she stands within destruction. She realised that her life had lost its meaning. She built her courage up, as she learnt about self-love. She lived in the shadow of another for so long that she truly had enough.

She knew that he was wrong, but she was scared of loneliness and what would happen after love. That's the problem with staying stuck. You want to believe every word and every lie, but then you lose yourself with time. There came a day when he pushed too hard, and she couldn't take the ache. She was tired of repeating the same mistakes. She knew she had to leave her love behind, because at this point, there was no love to find. It takes a lot of strength to be able to change your mind when your thoughts are built on lies.

He promised he'd never hurt her anymore, as he made the same remarks that she once knew. Her tolerance was slipping, and she could sense his untold truth. She saw through every word and every kiss. He made her feel grotesque. He slashed her heart into this shade of blue, when she was never one to be untrue. She said goodbye to misery, as she walked out of the door. She never once turned back to see his heart of stone. She fought a war of agony and found herself healing insecurities. There may be no such thing as happiness, but her smile returned to what it used to be.

Broken Pages

The fear of yesterday

We're never quite sure where life will take us, or what we'll someday lose. We always want to plan the future but fall short on having any clue. We let the hours pass, as we age away from what we knew. We're made to be persistent, even when we're slowly fading. There's an emptiness inside me and it never seems to sleep. I've felt these words before in a different time and place, but they never fed my soul to assist me with escape. I've always wanted to run away; to find somewhere new where no one knows my name. I guess it's what we do. We look for scenery that forces us to change. We're terrified of life and the numbness it contains. We never want to be the same, as we try to fight the pain. We're lost within thoughts that keep us in the dark, as the silence still remains. We're a different shade of broken when we live in fear of yesterday.

The regret we feel is never-ending. It's sad. It really is. We move further along our lives, yet we're standing within a death of time. We're pulled towards our memories more than moments that transpire. The only light ahead of us is one that paints a story of disaster, as we feel the future's too hard for us to reach. There's a sadness deep inside me, and it fills me up with guilt. I'm tainted by the past and all these barriers I built. I keep searching for a friend, but no one seems to hear me when I'm screaming within myself. Please don't leave. I'm

Broken Pages

begging you to stay as my thoughts start to drift away. This is me without dishonesty and a lack of empathy.

I always lived within the past, wondering who I am. I never truly saw myself as anything close to what you see today. It took some time to realise that I let myself decay. I would stare out into space, wondering what it is I'm doing or if I'll ever be someone worth remembering. I turned these pages of my story, but they were blank in their entirety. I was lost within what used to be, even in my fear of yesterday. It pulled me back considerably, as I gave into the cold without a sense of dignity. I wanted to be connected to a mind that I neglected, but all I ever did was think to a point where none of me was perfect.

I had a dream that tomorrow would somehow help me shine, but that has always been my biggest lie. I've been going backwards all my life, as I try to fight to somehow feel alive. I've never had the strength to say goodbye, even to the ones who left my side. I'm attached to stories I once told, as if I'm slightly glued to a past that I once held. There's a madness deep inside me, and it pulls me from the surface. It's as if I'm drowning where water isn't present, and these words are all that suffocate my breathing. I'm attracted to being broken and it seems to be my burden. I carry scars across my head and chest, as I try to claw my way out of this mess. I've been holding hope for something better, but as the days go on, my heart feels colder. I'm disconnected from everything I feel, because I view the world as nothing more than hell. It's a sad truth that I try my best to never tell. I'm running out of happiness, and it seems to be affecting me. I'm just tired, you know? I've been on this road for so long that it feels like I'm repeating the same old song.

I let myself fall into places that prevented me from healing. I was never quite sure of who I was, or if I'll ever find myself beyond these scars. They were part of my existence that only made me see my life as colourless. There's a beating heart inside me, and it's rapidly declining. We never realise what our hearts are doing, and behind the scenes mine was slightly breaking. I remember how it felt to feel alive, but all this beauty had faded into nothing, as every fibre of my being had somehow been dismantled. It's sad. It really is. I never saw myself as damaged until I realised tomorrow never came. I was standing still within my fear of yesterday.

I sometimes speak without a thought inside my head. It's as if I'm vacant yet still able to somehow walk ahead. If words could paint a vivid picture, I'd paint the skies with stories of a missing future. I never feel like I do anything that benefits the person I was meant to be. I wanted to resemble the one inside the mirror staring back at me. We belong to no one other than ourselves, and we forget that at times, because we're drawn to what we left behind. We hurt ourselves more than those who infect our minds, yet we place the blame on others, because we're scared to be responsible. I knew the

Broken Pages

problems had gone away, yet the memories still remained. It never occurred to me that I refused to change. You see, I kept thinking, and I kept thinking until the fear I had was somewhat buried. We always have a choice yet never seem to see it. We lack clarity of what could be when we're reminded of what was. I was tired of being wasted. I just needed to find peace within my tragedies.

We search for answers every single night, as the past creeps into our minds. We want to forgive and forget, but all we do is prevent ourselves from moving. The saddest story ever told is the one we tell ourselves. It hurts, you know? We live for so little, yet we're stuck inside a cycle. I really wish that you could see what I see, because then you'd understand me. I always lived in fear of yesterday, but trauma is something we all go through. We lose our smiles so easily. It's saddening. The problem is we never write tomorrow, so we stay still within the past until we fade into our shadows. I never want to feel that fear again. I never want to wake up feeling restless. I want to rule the world, even if it's all inside my head. This is goodbye to the chains that held me still. I'm taking back the person that you stole.

The lies I tell myself

I whisper in the air that everything is fine, as I pull the curtain one last time. These are the lies I tell myself when I'm in denial. I drown out every truth in a fabricated style. It's what I do to ease the pain of life. I wish someone could see me behind my weary smile. I wrote a thousand letters, depicting everything I've felt. I wanted to reach out and grab you by the heart strings to play you like a violin. I'm not an artist or clairvoyant; I'm a human being. It isn't an easy statement to admit. We want to be more than human, because we feel like we're afflicted. We never want to own up to the truth of what is, because we're drawn to the falsities of life. The lies I used to tell myself are still lingering inside my mind. I thought that I was flawless, but that was part of my demise. I never knew how hard I'd fall by opening my eyes.

We're slightly blind. Maybe by design. We want to see things clearly, but always blur the lines. I used to be afraid of emptying my mind until suddenly these words became my life. I never understood what I was doing. I never had a plan. I never felt like I was growing, and maybe I never had a chance. I kept pretending that I could smile, but I guess it was a lie I'd tell myself to sleep at night. I always wished that I could sleep, but these nightmares would claw into my skin and I would feel them cut me deep. I'm a product of the cold. The one I always mention when I'm expressing why I'm broken. It's that side of me that hurts, even when I'm far away and dreaming. I always feel alive yet dead, as my heart is rapidly beating to the sound of words I left unsaid. These are the lies I tell myself to help me with my breathing. I just wish you'd understand these words that I've been leaving. They're the answers that you need, but only if you completely give your soul to me.

I wish I could be perfect, but these flaws keep staring back at me. They took away my innocence. They turned me into Papikins, and oh my god, it hurts me when I sin. I fill my mind with disaster, as I go through all the motions in my time of overthinking. I just want to make sense of what I'm given, but these roads lead me to depression. I used to be so distant then I came across the sun, and I felt like I was lifted. We hide ourselves away, wondering when it's time to reappear, because we never truly disappear. We want to, but we don't. We let ourselves fade into the moon, as the night is where we mostly feel like we're bleeding blue.

There's this sadness in our eyes that never seems to let us go. It suddenly hurts to be alive, as we somehow find ourselves crawling on the floor. We feel as though it's over, but the pain has just begun. That's the sad reality of feeling like you're numb. You know that pain exists, but you hurt more than what you want. We always tell each other that we're empty, or that we feel absolutely nothing. That's a lie we tell ourselves to avoid the problems that we're facing. We just want the world to see us smiling, but on the inside, it fucking feels like we're almost dying. It's hard to read these words and not think about yourself. We always push for something, yet when we fail, we feel our worlds are crumbling. We never have the courage to say it like it is, so we lie, and we lie, until there's nothing left to give. We lose our value. We lose everything that makes us real.

There have been times where I've tried to cut away the pain, but all I ever did was help these demons stay. We assume that removing what we feel will somehow save us from ourselves, not realising that we accelerate the ache. We never treat ourselves correctly. We place pressure on our souls to change. We're begging to be a different person, but even then, we'll still feel as though we're breaking. We're never satisfied with our reflections. We wake to sleep, and we sleep to wake. It's as if we're made to repeat the same mistakes. It isn't easy to admit when you're lying to yourself. You make excuses to stay complacent. You want to feed your soul but never leave your comfort zone. I do it all the time. I'm just scared of what will happen if I amount to nothing.

I keep thinking, and I keep thinking until these scars have healed completely. There's never any reason to keep yourself from living. The lies I told myself were only stopping me from growing. We have a fear of overthinking, but I live for the adrenaline. I love each and every feeling. We barely give ourselves any space for growth. We always fear for the worst. I want you to realise that everything that happens is a chapter in your story and the outcome is never written. We lie to keep our sanity, but in the end, we break too easily, as if we're made of porcelain. I hope you find your honesty, and honestly, you're a broken shade of beautiful to me.

Monster

There comes a time where you'll feel at your lowest. Believe me, I know it. You'll feel empty and weak. You'll feel like your world is suddenly closing, and you can barely even speak. I feel for you. I truly do. Hurt is temporary. What you feel today, you won't feel tomorrow. We refuse to see it that way, because we're scared to open up to change. We're afraid that we'll let go of all the familiar things we love, so we stay. We stay in places that we hate, and we never seem to stop. We're drawn to emotions that only hurt us. We do it to defend ourselves from loss. We lose ourselves so easily. It's sickening. We place our trust in life as if it was made to help us fight. It isn't. We fight for ourselves and that's the bitter truth that most of us will hide.

I was tired of life and what it did to me. I was searching for nothing, but never even knew it. I would hold on for too long. It was something I was never proud of, but even when our minds are begging us to change, we never want to. I woke up wondering who I am, because I was always stuck inside of who I used to be. I knew I had to find a way to push through whatever life had given me. I didn't want to be afflicted any longer. I wanted to feel more human rather than a fucking monster.

The fall

We run away from feelings that we deem as unacceptable. We want the world to perceive us as if we have control. We're in dire need of change, but we can't cope with losing out on familiar things. It's a weakness that stops us from achieving all our dreams. There were times where I would fall but lacked the will to stand back on my feet. I would cry myself to sleep, wondering why I find it hard to breathe. I would have these conversations with myself that made me wish that I was someone else. My courage was non-existent, as I fell into depression. I was always scared that it would happen. You can feel it, you know? You can feel the dark cloud over your head as it covers you in dread.

 I knew there was something wrong but found it hard to communicate the way I felt. I wanted to release the anger and the pain to self-medicate my guilt. I knew that no one else could help, and it was cutting at my heart. I was tired of feeling less when all my love was gone. I was drowning in my sorrows, as the world would move without me. I didn't understand how I was meant to feel. I was captivated by the thought of dying, but somehow, I knew that my life would have more meaning. I would let the hours pass, as the darkness turned my shadow into nothing. I sat there without hope, trying to figure out where I was going. I would look outside and think that this world isn't somewhere I belong. My existence was in question. I had this endless need to hide,

Broken Pages

because I felt that I was bound to be imperfect. I placed too much importance on perfection, because I hated to see myself fall victim to rejection. I avoided life and all its mysteries, because I was scared that I would never be satisfied completely.

The days would turn to weeks, as the weeks would turn to months. I shed tears, as the months turned into years. The voice inside my head would always keep me up. It wanted me to separate the part of me that feels from the part of me that aches. I knew that life was full of failure, but I guess I couldn't face it. There was so much that I wanted to erase, and it got to a point where reality was twisted. I would stare at my reflection and wonder what happened to my face. My smile was slowly shifting, and I found it hard to fake. I hated everything about my smile, because no one knew the pain that I hid beneath it. I fought for years with overthinking. It pushed me further to the thought of ending things. I'm not proud of what it is I'm writing, but this is the reason why I love the thought of breaking. This is the reason why I'm the broken king. I held the world inside my hands, and I felt these worries slip between my fingers. I finally saw everyone around me for who they are and will be. I was hurting every single night, trying to make sense of this wretched plight. I knew that in the end, everything would somehow be alright.

I effortlessly moved from one thought to another, and it was scarier than anything I've previously encountered. I remember the pounding in my head, as I tried to change my train of thought. I wanted to be real in a sea full of venom, but

Broken Pages

these demons wouldn't stop asking me to save them. I was caught up in how I felt and what I lost. My world became a tragedy that I knew was less than ordinary. I had to give in to the cold to see the problems I was hiding. I became a little more observant, and suddenly this pain had quietly been lifted. I was moving too fast to even register what was going on around me. I had to slow the world down to feel like I was free. I never understood why I felt so lonely, but as the years would pass, I could see it clearly. We were born to be alone, but we find others to be alone with. Some of them may not even fit, but we're lonely with each other. It's the reason why we feel detached within the company of others. It's normal. It's part of being human. I cried these tears for too long to even be remembered. I was tired of searching for connection when I found I may not even need it. That's the problem that I had before this; I would always look at life like it was built on complex theories.

I'm an overthinker. I take every piece of this scattered story and fit them all together. I connect these parts of life and try to make sense of what I'm given. It used to hurt to be this damaged, but that's a label that others would assign me. I was tired of living in a world of make-belief, scouring for hope that I would find a purpose. The truth is that life is what we make it. I was on the verge of disappearing. I know it's hard to breathe when you feel like you're constricted, but sometimes, you have to realise that life is too short to be stuck within your self-created boundaries. I now know that falling will always be a part of me. It's part of every move I make, as I move across my story.

A hundred days

There I go, pacing back to hell. There are so many stories that I have to tell. I hide each and every one from these prying eyes, because they won't understand the damage that's been done. I used to walk beside you, but now I walk alone. It feels like a hundred days have passed, but it's been a thousand more. I had a grasp of time, but now the hours fade as quickly as my mind. I remember us like yesterday. These feelings still remain, and every memory lingers in my head, as I try my best to finally forget. We were so close yet so far, like a shooting star. You were the dream that kept on giving, until you broke my world apart.

    The darkest days have come and gone, yet I still feel like everything is wrong. I tried to breathe without you, but I thought emotions stay the same. I couldn't keep on lying, because I was destroying everything I built. I would fall at every aspect of what we used to have, and as to be expected, I would override my feelings with a sense of guilt and hatred. That's the problem that I had. I would focus on the past. I would look at all these pictures, in hopes that I would find a way out of my collapse. I had nothing left to give. I had nothing left to say. I hurt myself with thoughts of us, because I never knew that a hundred days would pass. I was trapped within my mind, as I saw no urgency in time. I captured all these moments without a sense of sadness. I felt alive and lost in the memories of us. I wanted to belong without warmth, but my heart suddenly ran cold.

Broken Pages

I was torn apart by love and left here with these scars of us. It felt like minutes passed, yet the moon had come and gone. I was stuck inside our forever after, and what came after you was silence and disaster. I kept thinking, and I kept thinking until I overthought. Our ending was one I never truly planned. The idea of love was something that I cherished, but all these flowers that had bloomed had suddenly all wilted. I apologise if you wanted me to be in stasis, but I found the strength to fight it. A hundred days have passed, but this is my goodbye to the thousands that will never come to be.

Until my breath escapes me

I'm shaking at the fear of dying. I have this feeling of regret inside me, and it's only getting worse. This constant search for happiness is driving me insane. How can I be happy with myself when depression rules above all else? I write the saddest lines, pretending that I'm fine. Nothing seems to help. I tried to medicate these demons, but they were only sleeping. Do you understand me? Do any of you truly understand what's behind these words that I've been screaming? It goes through my head on a daily basis, and I hope that you can see this.

The thing with me is that I keep breathing, and I keep breathing until my breath escapes me. Every feeling is a memory. Every sentence is someone I held closely, but now I'm back to being lonely. I'm fading away from this life that I created, and I'm turning into someone I once hated. There's such beauty to these words inside my head, and they're wasted on someone who would rather hurt instead. I'm always hurting, and that's the secret to my success. I never knew how to put these words together, but I wanted to make sense of everything that I could possibly remember. I'm an overthinker, it's what I do best when I'm around something that resembles pen and paper. I breathe words as if they're fire, and let you into a damaged reality where I'm the broken king that you admire. I set out to give a voice to those who hurt, and in the process, I lost myself instead.

I always believed in fairy tales, but now I'm not too sure that they exist. I saw the tragedies I left behind and somehow questioned why I'm still alive. I was so afraid of breathing, because I knew that it would ultimately hurt me. Why do I keep wondering if anyone understands this? Of course, you do. We're connected after all. I am you, and you are me. Isn't it wonderful? We're the reality of being human. We don't find escape in false messages that try to inspire hope, because we know that we were made to be alone. I know you want to be a perfect soul but let me tell you something; it doesn't exist. I'm sorry. I'm just a realist.

Broken Pages

My heart bleeds blue

There are days where I've spiralled into madness. I've fought a war that's everlasting. I used to see brighter days ahead, but they've gradually been fading. I'm a disaster full of worry, but these faults are not the only woe I carry. I have a secret that I've been hiding, and it's time for me to tell the truth. My heart bleeds blue. I used to wish that I could fly, but these wings would never grow. I used to see the earth from a narrow point of view, but now I see the universe, and it's reminding me of you. This is what it means for someone's heart to turn into a broken shade of blue. The worst part of me has seemingly always been you. I hope you understand what I mean, as I stare into the reflection of my screen. I'm afraid of all these thoughts. I'm afraid of being here alone, drowning within this emptiness I lost.

I bleed into these pages as I watch the world around me. I could never understand why my flame expired. I was shining brightly underneath the surface, but deep down I lacked empathy and purpose. I spent my lonely nights wondering how it felt to be more human, as I rearranged these thoughts of anguish. The worst part about being an overthinker is that you want to make sense of everything that you remember. You keep thinking, and you keep thinking until you slowly start to lose your smile. I never wanted it to happen, but I guess everything has its reasons. There was nothing I could do to stop myself from thinking; it's part of being human. The problem with me is that I never feel satisfied with anything I do. I'm always aiming to be a better person, but feel worse when my dreams are shattered. I have this need to feel alive but end up grieving over the death of time. The words I write are nothing in my eyes. It's something I must live with and bottle up inside.

I never had the courage to expose myself as much as I had wanted. I thought people would stare at me with hatred. I thought these broken pieces would push me towards the edge where escape was not an option. These words are merely self-expression, but why do they feel like they're voiced by another person? That's the beauty behind observance. I combine my world with others and somehow let what we share pour into all these broken pages. I'm an overthinker created from disaster. I had to be this person. I had to expand my intuition just to breathe life into these situations.

I always knew that I would end up here alone. I remember love and what it did to me. What a fucking tragedy. I remember who I was before the pain began to settle in, and who I became when my heart began to sink. There was nothing more daunting than finding out I had no hand to hold. It hit me hard, as I gave in to the cold. It was never my intention to fall in love so deeply. We can't control our feelings, and that's the sad reality. I had nowhere else to go to, other than a path of solitude, as I lost the better part of me. I knew it had to happen, but I was still surprised by the dreaded outcome. I knew that loneliness would stare at me again, as I fought with myself until the bitter end. I was walking blindly into the fire, punishing myself for losing the only person I desired. It's love, I guess. We take it all for granted, as our happiness cascades into nothingness instead. It's how it's always been, yet we find it hard to comprehend.

I struggled to make sense of why I felt so broken. I knew my heart was caving, but the stiffness was alarming. My chest was frozen still, and the grip was slowly tightening. I could suddenly feel silence, as I lost the fuel that burnt the fire that's inside me. It was then I knew that my heart would forever bleed the deepest shade of blue. The saddest stories are always told by those who smile. I would always let my laughter linger, because I never wanted to remember. I couldn't close my eyes for longer than a second, because I would fall into a nightmare. It was as if these dreams had faded, and darkness was a newfound friend of mine. I had no one left to stop me from giving in to my broken mind. These thoughts were pushing me towards surrender, and I somehow knew that it would happen. It's a flaw within my sanity that's been somehow killing me. I expect the worst from everyone. I always ruin everything. It's the reason why I'm writing, to apologise for being me and falling in love without accepting my insecurities.

The most tiring feeling in the world is to love. You give yourself away so easily, as you feel a sensation that burns you to the touch. You run away with ideas of being happy, but suddenly, you fall victim to letting go of who you are. The burn begins to alter, as the frostbite settles in. The fire you once knew becomes ice within your soul, as it sets you up to fall. You wonder why you were chosen for this fate. You never wanted it to be, but it becomes all you ever know. You're lost. You're afraid. You've made so many careless mistakes, and you know it. You know deep down that it'll never go away. You blame yourself for a situation you feel you could have prevented. I feel for you. I truly do, because this is how it was for me.

It's rough. It really is. We hold ourselves accountable for mostly everything we do. If we can't find happiness, then we feel as though these colours have turned to blue. We bleed relentlessly until the only option left for us is to lose. It's a sad situation, and it only opens up our self-created wounds. There's nothing we can do to take the ache away. That's the saddest truth that most of us evade. We're scared of what could happen if we submit to overthinking, but no one understands it. They say it's more of a curse than it is a blessing, but here I am the broken artist. I give meaning to everything I write because I want to feel more human. I want to be able to think freely without constraint. I want to hurt on my own terms rather than letting others fill me with regret. I never truly understood what it meant to be immersed within existence until the aftermath of love. It's sad. It really is. I had to break apart to breathe.

I held on to every lie, as I sat and stared at love's demise. I thought the world was crumbling, not knowing it was only mine. I was walking in the shallow end of water, but I somehow fell and drowned. I was a product of the broken, yet never knew exactly what it meant to actually be open. I still remember how it felt when my heart didn't bleed this shade of blue. I fight the pain away every single day. I know that I'd be going backwards if my mind wandered into thoughts of you. You were everything to me. You were the reason why I wanted to succeed. I thought I needed you to prevent myself from repeating history. I was scared of losing the familiar feeling I once knew. I was amazed at how much I loved you, but through all the pain we put each other through, I'm sorry you never saw me the same as I saw you.

I finally saw the lies behind your eyes, as I kept our love alive. It's the worst feeling to have when you know you face impending doom, and I could feel the tension loom. I was afraid of the future. I was afraid of letting go of what we had, but people grow apart, even if it's sad. I was in love with this idea that I created, and I still feel as though we could have made it. There was a glimmer of hope some days, but the possibilities were slim, as I held on to a tearing string. I was pulling on it in hopes that I could save us, but it came to nothing. I'll repeat every single word until it makes a little sense. I wanted to be happy in an empty universe for one, but it was hard to do when I remember having you.

I was putting too much trust into my heart yet always seemed to fill my head with empty promises. I wrote your name a thousand times until I had no reason to. That's the part of love and loss that gives me meaning, and the reason why my heart is bleeding. I chose to accept that I was broken. No one ever seems to tell you that acceptance leads you to a place of overthinking, and that's exactly what had happened. I opened up my mind to what it means to feel more vividly, as I drew these moving pictures with words that transformed into chaotic poetry.

The world is made of stories that most of us have lived through. Sometimes it's hard to accept that another feels your pain. We hurt so easily. We're fragile in our separate shades of broken. I wanted to be beautiful. I wanted to find a reason to see a different colour other than this wretched blue, but I couldn't. It was the only thing that kept me sane. I was stranded in the ocean all alone, contemplating on my broken thoughts. I had to douse away the ache until the cold had taken over. I thought it was the only way to stop myself from bleeding, but sadly, I created more problems with my change in thinking. I never expected to be this distant, but I had nothing left to lose, so I gave in to the cold until my heart bled blue.

Just breathe

Just breathe. It takes a while to catch your breath again, and sometimes we forget that. We dream of a better tomorrow but lack an understanding of what it means to live within today. It's as if we're destined to be human for all our lives. We're ordinary people made to make mistakes, but why does it hurt knowing that we're not special? I'm not going to lie to you. Not today. We build ourselves with distractions, as we waste our lives away. It's a sad truth that we never seem to see. We over-analyse the world around us, and we never seem to breathe. It's part of why we fail when we desperately long to heal. That's the problem that we have with life. We wonder why we hurt, but never assess the reasons why we burn. Believe me when I tell you that everything around you is never what it seems. You assume the worst in people, as you build a wall to keep you safe. It's how it is when we feel afraid. We fear the worst is yet to come, as our breath seems to slip away.

Broken pages

I've been fighting off temptations to let go of my existence. It's hard for me to communicate with family and friends, because I'm afraid of what they'll think of me. I'm slowly going through these changes no one seems to see. I don't feel human or anything in between as I ink these broken pages. I wanted to salvage the better parts of who I used to be, but couldn't find anything to keep. I'm so fucking tired of feeling like a burden. I'm tired of looking into the mirror and wondering why I'm hurting. I haven't cried for months, yet I feel like my heart's been bleeding. I've struggled with a disease many label as overthinking. I seem to set the world on fire with these thoughts that cut my breathing.

    I have a constant tension in my chest that only leaves me with unrest, and it's been a while since I've felt alive within the universe. I'm the victim, villain, saviour, and witness all at once yet rarely feel like I exist. The simple things in life are the ones we take for granted. I've been writing to release, yet it hurts as each word is splattered to these pages. I always looked for peace in strange places, but all I ever found were my scattered pieces. I thought I could fix them, but sadly, they were chapters in my story. They were me in my entirety yet displaced within this tragedy. These lines are poetically pathetic, yet eerily aesthetic. I ponder what is left when I finally reach my writer's death.

Distractions

I always speak about myself yet rarely think of others. It's clearly part of my destruction. I never want to know anyone for who they are, because I'm scared of who they'll eventually become. The truth is that I promised myself I'll withdraw from friendly interaction, because I'm addicted to distraction. You see, we lower down our walls in hopes of letting others into our self-created worlds. We're constantly searching for matching souls. We want them to understand us even when we're quiet, because that's the purest form of connection if I'm honest. There are times when we break and seek for comfort. Those are the times when we need ourselves the most, but we take our chances in trusting external forces. We're conditioned to believe that happiness is something we achieve. It isn't. I'm sorry if I let you down, but honestly speaking, this is why I wear my broken crown. I would always look towards the skies and wonder why it hurts to be here; why I feel disconnected from my peers. I wanted to blend in with the crowd, but never realised I wouldn't be the person I am now.

There's an emptiness to feeling broken, I guess. We form our thoughts without dishonesty, because we're more inclined to be truthful when we're left with nothing. We want to be seen as lively when inside we're slowly dying. It's as if we want someone to truly see us, but we refuse to admit we crave affection. We hide behind the falsities of life, as we try to keep our distance. It feels wrong being close to one another knowing that our paths may one day falter. I want everything to be beautiful. I want to cover all these scars without restriction, because I'm fucking tired of being censored. The older that I get, I realise these stories built me into who I am today. I never allowed myself to be fully present. I was too scared to fade within these dreams that I was chasing. I was nothing more than vacant, as I rode the stars into the ocean. I fell into the blue because I gave myself away.

How does it feel to know you hurt me? That was a question I would ask myself repeatedly. I tried to find the answer, but never gave myself any space to breathe. It's the worst mistake I ever made. I was pretending to be happy, as I put myself last in everything I did. I always wanted to be alone, but these demons screamed within my head. I'm the worst kind of person. I'm an overthinker made to bleed. We fall apart in pieces, as we live and learn the vanities of brokenness, and to be quite honest, it's what makes us monstrous. We strive to understand the reasons why we place our trust within distractions, but never learn from the thoughts that we possess. It's part of being human that none of us are willing to confess.

I've always been attracted to getting closer, but I have a problem with easily being used somewhere in the future. We rely on attachment to somehow fix ourselves. We hold on to people that never feed our souls. We overthink the world and what it is, but never live within the present, because it's too hard for us to grasp. It's as if we're made to be exploited. It's as if the moments that we form are made of loss and emptiness. We keep thinking, and we keep thinking until we hurt inside. It's all we seem to do, as we wonder what it means to be alive. Every stranger that we meet stays a stranger in our lives, and it's pretty hard to handle when we crave to love and be adored.

We fool ourselves wholeheartedly, as we crash into the haze. We want those surrounding us to stay until the end of days; friends, family, and lovers that scratch our hearts away. We make the same mistakes because we're destined to be human. We're vulnerable and empty but fill ourselves with lies. It's how everything was made to be yet what we fail to see. We set the bar high for one another, not knowing that we're on a road to failure. That's the saddest part of human nature. We long to find connection, as we draw beliefs from picture perfect visions. You see, expectations were made to kill, and our stomachs can clearly tell. We suddenly feel faint when perfection can't ever be attained. It's how our stories go, as we rip apart our souls.

There are a thousand ways to die, but what kills us is whatever lurks within our minds. We have a constant stream of thoughts that we'd rather turn to silence. We sense that we're hardly speaking, but these voices sleep within us. We hold them hostage because we're afraid of saying truths that'll only hurt us. Why do we feel the way we do? Why do we put emphasis on emotions that fail to stay within existence? We wander all across our minds, as we try to get a glimpse of the past that always felt unkind. We over feel and overthink yet are influenced by forces that only leave. We want to please people as much as possible, just to feel relieved. We were made to believe that selflessness would save us, but eventually we become broken in the process. It's a sad truth that we refuse to see, because we're scared of living life more selfishly.

Where does the madness end? We feel the need to give ourselves away to each and every friend. We set ourselves up to fall back down again. Everyone suddenly becomes a stranger when life begins to change. There comes a time when the people around us start to slowly drift away. The bitter truth is that our paths begin to part, as we find less reasons just to stay. The problem with being there for everyone is that it causes us to break. We forget about life entirely, as we narrow down the roads available to take. It's how it seems to be when we go from A to B. We hold on to familiar faces to prevent ourselves from drowning. We can't possibly let go of the ones we seem to know, even though they bring us down towards a six foot hole.

Beyond my broken crown

I'm drowning in my thoughts and I've seen these visions once before. They remind me of places that I've been and faces that I've lost. I dream about them relentlessly, as I scream within my sleep. These nightmares are recurring. They form the broken crown I'm wearing. I've been down too many roads, and they've led me to a path of overthinking. Isn't it amazing? I overthink the little things. You know, the ones that cut into your skin, as you hide away your sins. I seem to love to hurt myself. It truly isn't my intention. I've been walking around the world without a sense of empathy. It might be the reason why I disconnect so easily. I don't understand what people expect of me. I can't be the perfect person they envision. It isn't my style to want to achieve higher than my own limits.

It's sad, isn't it? I've been living within these boundaries, as I move the world around me. It's the fault that I've been living with throughout this life of misery. I guess it's just a part of me. I have these thoughts that never leave. They pound into my head like I'm staring at the sun, and it grows stronger as the days go on. I'm tired of satisfying others' needs before my own. I'm a beautiful creation. That's what everybody says, but they don't truly know me. We never know each other as well as we might think. We have these different faces, and our masks are too heavy to be lifted. We show a part of us that we're screaming out to be. I know you feel it too, don't lie to me. We sit there among our friends and family, as we try to understand the reasons why we feel detached. It isn't because we're empty, it's because we break apart too easily, and that's the sad reality.

We're fragile beings made to tear into smaller pieces of who we used to be. There's no denying it. We feel the need to put ourselves in places that no one ever wants to. Is it because we lack self-belief? I know it all too well. I hurt myself at times, because I felt unworthy of living life. I knew I was going nowhere, but I had to figure out a way to get there. You see, that's the part of stories we never dare to ask. We always want to know the why, rather than the how. I was putting all these thoughts into being happy. I wanted to be normal, but normality was never in my reach. I could tell a thousand lies, but one truth would hurt the most. I was hiding in the shadows, pretending everything was fine. The truth is that it never was. I never felt like I could fly, and there were days where I barely felt alive.

I would stare out into space to look up at the stars and wonder how they came to be. I wanted to be up there in the skies. I wanted to steal their sparkle and their shine. I knew I had a thousand problems, but I wanted to feel like I was worth it. How do I say this without breaking? I wanted to push away these thoughts that left me shaking. I never felt like much, and that was pushing me away from everyone I knew. I was finding it hard to be myself, as I struggled to find my purpose. I hated all the memories I had, because they damaged me inside. I was looking for validation in all the wrong places. I had to be accepted, no matter how much it hurt for me to change. I never knew that I'd replace the pain with guilt. It was out of my control. I wanted to be happy in a world I called my own.

There was a moment in time where I felt like everything was crumbling. I wanted to get better, but sometimes nothing goes to plan. These words swirled around my tongue, as I whispered to myself. The thoughts were slowly flooding, as I let them out without a sound. I couldn't stop myself from thinking. It felt like my mind was surely burning. I guess that's how I became the broken king. I was dreaming while awake, and every fibre of my being was telling me that I was growing empty. I could feel a side of me that I never felt before. I was scared that everything would end, but these pictures I once knew were shifting in my head. I could rearrange the pieces, but eventually I hurt. Every night was made to be a struggle, as I thought to a point of no return.

The broken parts of me were suddenly appearing, and my grip on reality was slightly fading. The pain was overbearing, so I would cry myself to sleep, if only I could sleep. I would lie awake at night, thinking about the reasons why nothing feels alright. I wanted to let go, and that's the honest truth. I had nothing left to show. I was falling down my self-created hole, and I was exhausted of being reminded that I've lost control. You see, it isn't easy being broken. You put your faith in those around you, but will they be there when you ultimately fall? I could never trust anyone, because I couldn't trust myself. This plague within my mind was rushing through my veins. I felt disconnected all the time, as

Broken Pages

I gave in to the pain. I was afraid of life and death, but never had the chance to live or die. I was only wasting breath.

Do you know how it feels to be lost? I was roaming around limbo, trying to put these pieces back together. These thoughts were increasing my anxiety. I found it hard to communicate, because no one would understand me. My vision was distorted, and every face was far and distant. I couldn't see people the way I used to. My perception wouldn't let me. I could see behind their smiles, and it led me into tragedy. The worst part about being broken is that I see others behind the skin they live in. I somehow notice every fear that they've been hiding, and the cracks that they leave showing. I see their insecurities looking back at me, and I always hoped to God that they would see me too. I never thought that I would be like this. I'm a broken mess of brokenness, and I'll keep repeating it until I rest.

I would always focus on the bad rather than the good. It was a part of me I never understood. There were times where everyone would tell me to be more optimistic, but they never knew what was underneath the surface, as I battled with regret that made me feel so hopeless. I wanted nothing more than to be alive in a world full of dread and darkness. That's the problem with being someone like me. There's nothing wrong but nothing right. You're in a paralysed state of sadness. It catches up with you from time to time, and it's hard to process. I was living without an urgency to do anything than just be. Do you understand how bad that is? I was living just to live rather than wanting more from life than

Broken Pages

what I had. It slowed me down in everything I did. I was never motivated to succeed. I never felt like I could reach anywhere other than the bottom, because it was all I ever knew.

The worst was yet to come, as I trusted in my heart and gave myself to love. I remember everything so vividly. I remember you and what you did to me. It was the weakness that I always knew I had. I wanted to be less lonely. I wanted to be able to smile and live a life of honesty, and honestly, I thought the world of you. The truth is that romance is dead. It died a long time ago. It died when our worlds had slowly parted, even if I felt as though we never truly started. I was always in love with the idea of being loved. I was always alone and yearning to be touched, not physically, but mentally. I wanted to share this broken side of me with someone else, however selfish that may be. I never knew the destructive nature of how I felt. I never wanted to love; I was just desperate to feel. I didn't want to fall back to these thoughts of panic. I knew that everything would push me towards a broken ending.

I needed you to save me. I needed you to tell me that everything will be fine, because I wasn't. I was holding back the tears, as I dreamt about your smile and thought about your voice. I was fading from reality, or so it seemed. I couldn't keep going on without you. It's as if this hurt was amplified, as I moved across the chapter that erased you from my life. I needed a sign that I'll be alright. The moment I lost you is one that's hard to comprehend. I was searching for an answer but disregarded the ones that I refused to hear. It's as if I was determined to find one that's far away from the truth. These walls were closing in, as I kept myself standing still. I wish I knew the reason why you left, but it doesn't feel that real. I guess that was my problem. I never saw reality the way that others did. I covered up our love with lies to hold on to the past to help me heal.

I've been pushing life away, as I live without you every day. I'm spiralling out of control, and I don't think you'd like the change. You left me with this hole that's leading me astray. These thoughts of happiness and love are an empty dream to me. I've put effort into being, yet I feel like a ghost with barely any meaning. It must be the loneliness that has me speaking, because before this, it was your light that kept me breathing. These words are laced with poetry, but the lines are less appealing. I played the victim well, as I tried to stop my heart from bleeding. I thought that I could get through the pain of love without truly understanding who I was, and who I truly am. There's a difference that many of us fail to see when it comes to self-perception. I guess that's why we're removed from our existence.

The problem with existing is that we depend on one another too much, too soon. We put our faith in temporary beings, as we light the path to each and every ending. I hope you understand that the world is full of sadness. I was trying to find peace out here by myself, as the brokenness increased when you left with someone else. I had nothing left to lose, yet everything to gain. I spent these lonely nights without you by my side, pretending to be fine. I needed someone there, but everyone was gone. The world came crashing down as I thought about your face, wondering why the earth was stuck beneath my feet. I knew I had to heal, but never had the will. The way our minds work after loss is tragically empty. We attach ourselves to sorrow, placing less importance on tomorrow. We hold our heads underneath the water, hoping to return to what we had before.

We're flawed as fuck, you know? We always try to save ourselves without understanding what it means to fall. We're scared of going back to being on our own. I was so fucking set on loving you forever, but here we are without each other. You were everything to me. You were the fire in my heart and the poison in my veins. You gave me hope and took it all away. I was so fucking lost without you and your embrace. I wanted to move on but hurt myself instead. I broke every part of me you fixed, and you know exactly what happened next.

The king of the broken

The saddest truths are the ones we hide away. We fear to be misheard, as we drown within mistakes. We're a different kind of breed. We're the broken beings that find it hard to breathe. There have been times where the world has closed in while I was growing, and my heart slightly just decayed. There's a repetition in my head, and it pulls me back to every word I ever said. I'm constantly concerned with the ideas that leave me speechless, because I want to understand the world and why I feel so distant. We sometimes live without a sense of purpose, so we try to find the answers. Why do we feel as though we're different? Where do we go when tomorrow isn't promised? You see, we keep thinking, and we keep thinking until the tides are breaking. We store these memories deep, as they haunt us when we sleep. It's as if we're prepared to meet defeat.

I've always been addicted to overthinking. I wanted it to heal me when nothing else ever did. It's hard to find acceptance when you rarely use your mind. You fall within distractions to fill yourself with silence. I wanted to stop pretending that everything was quiet. I felt it. I felt it in my dreams and loneliness. There was something there that gave me purpose. We never understand the reasons why we hurt. We were never meant to, I guess. We construct the past and what it did to us, yet we never seem to detach from the troubles that it caused. We're unable to let it go. The truth is that all of us are struggling. The pain is something we all live with, and some of us hide it better than the rest. We're unable to seek comfort because we fear that we'll be left with nothing. It's bullshit. We're beautiful within our brokenness, even if the world can't see it.

We let experiences ruin us. We let them sink into our skin, as we paint the stories out in ink. We seek for value in the company of others, but they become a burden when our paths eventually come towards the end. We mourn the loss of everyone we meet, even if they never leave. You can feel the disconnect. You can feel the emptiness that it creates. You fade into the darkness, as your memories are begging to be erased. I already told you that we were made for ruin. The truth is we let it happen. We let the thoughts control us rather than be the one with power. We're a different shade of beautiful, a broken one which nothing should control. It's never too late to embrace the person that's within. It's never too late to be proud of all your flaws. It's what I realised when I gave in to the cold.

We have this longing to be heard. We want to be seen as strong whenever we feel scared. It's a defensive way to be when you're hiding insecurities. We're our own worst enemies. We're exposed to our thoughts, and they lead us to abandon what is real. We critique ourselves based on everything we view, as we try to fit within society's ideals.

Broken Pages

We're drawn to belonging. It's a shame, because we'll never truly belong at all. I would always stare at people, wondering if I'll ever be their equal. I was stuck on the idea that I should be someone else instead. I hated my existence. I hated everything that I believed in, because I felt that no one would accept me. We all strive to be a perfect person, and I was far from perfect. I still am but my eyes are open now to see it.

A voice inside my head kept pushing me towards the edge. It never felt like me. I guess it was the person I always aspired that I would be. I knew perfection was non-existent. I knew that all my life I felt like I've been wasted. It was time for me to change my thinking. We always run from problems rather than stay and save ourselves from sinking. We always feel as though we lack the strength to stop our hearts from bleeding. The truth is I was strong enough to let mine bleed a broken shade of blue. It's the unknown, isn't it? We're unwilling to admit it, but we're scared of trying something new. We stay within the confines of our souls, as our minds are begging for reform. It's the reason why some of us will fall. We fight our thoughts until the bitter end, living life in all of its pretence.

We grow apart so easily. We roam around in misdirection, as we try to find the missing pieces. We always try to save ourselves by using other people. Maybe we're tired of being lonely creatures. Maybe it's beautiful to form connections. I would always hope that I would find salvation, but nothing seemed to calm my quiet storm, as I never knew exactly what it was that I was missing. There are a thousand ways to love yet most of us will falter when it comes to one. We lose ourselves within another's arms, as we leave the future with uncertainty. I dream about your face, whoever you are in this time and place. I believe that I will find you, somewhere in the cold and fall into your sweet embrace. The worst part about connection is that you never choose the ones you lose, but it hurts like hell when they fade into the blue. I've felt it all before. I know what it means to disconnect with someone that you once adored.

The damage we cause with love is sometimes seen as irreversible. We're more attached to heartbreak than we are with the one we lost. We're drawn to it so eerily, as it tears our lives apart. We're in a constant cycle of overthinking. It's sickening. We place our value on who we were before rather than learn how to let it go. We prevent our future growth. I wanted to be vulnerable. I wanted to shut out all the noise and be brave enough to turn these scars into something beautiful. There's a certain kind of beauty to sadness, but only if you see the world entirely. Sadly, some of us never do. We reject the idea that being broken could be beautiful, because of how it's treated by society.

The problem with existing in a world without ideas is that your mind becomes accustomed to a ubiquitous form of normalcy. You become too scared to leave the boundaries. It

Broken Pages

happens. We want to please the ones around us, even if it means we hide our true intentions. We never belong regardless. I thought I did, but it was never what I wanted. I was sick of being left behind. I was sick of feeling out of place wherever I would go. I needed somewhere safe to run, far away from the ones I only lie to. I had to keep thinking to a point of no return. I would quietly sit and stare at smiling faces all around me, but they were never happy. We're all afflicted by a certain kind of sadness, and as I put myself in restless situations, I could finally see beneath the masks of other people.

I want you to know the world is cruel, but if you forget that, you lose yourself entirely. I don't want to devalue anyone, because we all fight demons that scathe our souls at night. It's beautiful, isn't it? We run through problems in our heads as the pounding never stops. We feel as though we'll meet our end, but life keeps moving on. We overcomplicate our pain. We do it to ourselves, and that's the bitter truth. I want you to realise that we were made to break, but what's broken can never break again. We live to feel, and we feel to live. You may be losing hope, but you're still here. Our paths crossed to bring us to this point in time. I want you to understand that we are the broken. We are the ones who feel too much, too soon. We cry and we fall, but when we rise it's beautiful.

Entirety

We look at the world through blackened eyes and a darker soul. We expect to be given happiness in times where we feel like we're alone. We want to be real, but with reality comes pain. We feel the need to cover up our smiles, but the truth is that we go through the same mistakes. We're human and we're flawed. It's a sad truth that no one seems to tell you, as you push your sanity aside to reach a perfect soul. Is It truly perfect when perfection is non-existent? That's another mistake that reoccurs within our minds. We feel the pressure building up, but never let it go. We can't. It's not in our nature to do so. We're the broken beings of yesterday, because we fear to live within today. Do you know what I mean? It's sad. It really is. We never have a choice in anything we feel, or at least that's how it's perceived. You see, that's the reason why we break. We never have control. We let our minds wander off into a distant stream, until we're lost within our dreams.

I always had this nagging voice inside my head that would whisper pretty lies. I would call it a disease, but it was just the darkest side of me. It gave me false hope in a world that was closing in so rapidly. I was finding it hard to even calm myself when I was breaking, and boy oh boy, was I truly breaking. I was a star without its shine. I wanted to belong, not knowing it was nothing more than lies. Why do we feel this need to attach ourselves to others? I never understood it, and now I see it for what it is. We distract ourselves from being individuals. We're so afraid of seeing life without direction that we refuse to take on any chances that benefit our growth. It's a situation that I know a little bit too well. I trusted too much in everyone other than myself, and it goes to show when these lines are laced with poison and regret.

The way we move from one place to another is cruelty in its entirety. We're thrown into the world without any form of acceptance. It's difficult to breathe when we have a fear of being judged. We're always being scrutinised by others, but all of us do the same. It's part of humanity that no one can erase. We judge each other more than we can say. We let the past influence our thoughts, because we're afraid of living within today. It's that fear that drives us crazy, as we try to build the future. We always want to make it perfect, but somehow lose our senses. We're varied in our thoughts and feelings, but never dare to say it. We always want to be the better person, when in reality, we're wolves in sheep's clothing. I've seen it many times before; where the righteous cover up their flaws. They want to be adored, so they hide behind their plastered walls. They fear that they'll be scorned if anyone reveals their true intentions.

None of us are perfect. We're riddled with regret and masters of mistakes. There's no difference between being honest and being hurtful. I'm brutal when it comes to honesty, because honestly, I'm sick of liars and what they do to me. They put me in a position to feel more vividly, and when my visions become stronger than what my eyes can see,

Broken Pages

I lose myself entirely. We're attracted to lies to help us through the emptiness of life. I always wondered how people inspire each other without a sense of honesty. I'm sorry if you're vulnerable enough to need that kind of energy. It isn't something I'd recommend if you're feeling lonely. It only makes you worse to compare yourself to others. Believe me, I used to crave normality, but it wasn't what I expected it to be. I was desperately in need of saving, yet uninspired by optimistic imagery. The problem is that most of us will search for answers far and wide, but we create a sense of false hope that eats us up inside. I don't want to lie to you. I know how it feels to crave to be connected, but to be honest, forcing positivity will only ruin you.

I always thought about the world and why I felt so small. I couldn't bear to look at my reflection. I was scared I'd see another person. I was desperately trying to find salvation, but no one cared to give me hope. It's as if we're made to fall, yet some of us never get back up at all. We're the broken ones; the ones who feel too much, yet always seem to hide underneath a jaded smile. It's hard, isn't it? It's hard to know that somehow through all this silence, you can be labelled so fucking easily. I had this fear that cut me open. I was scared of all these possibilities. I was scared of looking at this glass and seeing it as empty. They always want to trick you into believing that half of it is there, when in reality, it's overflowing with beauty and despair. I used to believe in fairy tales. I used to wait for something better, but that pause in time would only hinder my progression. I was afraid of looking at the glass at all, yet never realised that it was mine

Broken Pages

to fill and throw away at will. We never truly understand the options that we have until we open up our minds.

I wanted success to somehow come towards me. I never accepted that fear controlled me. You see, we're too afraid to die so we never live at all. I was in that position for a while. I would wait for the days to pass, but each day would only be a waste. I would wait, and I would wait until another year had come and I had aged. I knew I would find my peace within this brokenness, even though others had despised it. I was tired of wasting time. I was tired of holding still when my mind was begging me to move. It was all I ever knew, and I guess that's how all of this had started. I had this fear of life that suffocated me into submission, but I knew that being broken would be my best decision. It's weird, isn't it? I thought I could turn the darkness into whatever it is that I desired. I put value into being fractured, as if it was my only calling. I hurt myself to a point of no return. I fed off this fear of loneliness, letting reality suddenly escape me. I had no reason to feel this lonely, but there I stood, trying to rid myself of happiness.

I never found an attraction to happiness like others do. It felt too forced to even be considered real. I couldn't see much behind depression as I lost myself in words. I could feel the silence linger, as my cries turned into lonely whispers. I felt the world around me moving, but I had thoughts of disappearing. I could never be satisfied, not even when imagining an ending. I neglected truths to maintain this sombre life that I've been living. I could tell you a thousand

Broken Pages

little things, but these words are all I have in these moments where I'm breaking. I knew the end would happen, but the journey is what intrigued me. I had my eyes closed for what felt like an eternity. These picture perfect dreams had become a vulnerability, and I wanted to find connection beyond what words could possibly describe. I wanted to be labelled as a monster. I wanted my humanity to be conquered. I wanted to finally win this self-inflicted plight. We refuse to see the truth sometimes, because it hurts us to know we're not alive.

I remember the first and last time I ever felt like I had died. I detached myself completely. I couldn't bear to be emotive. I couldn't understand it. I had so much hurt inside me. I had this unruly anger tearing me apart. There was a burning down my spine and a numbness in my heart, and somehow all these thoughts were gone. I thought I had fallen ill with emptiness. We always assume that being empty is a curse, but that's not entirely the truth. You have to fall down to your lowest to find yourself again. Believe me, I know it. I always wanted greatness. I always wanted to be happier than this, but the smiles were nothing more than lies, as I battled with my loneliness. You have to adjust to what you're given, as you cherish your existence. It's life. We hurt and we heal. There is no preventing the inevitable. We're broken shades of beautiful. Sometimes you have to stand in front of the mirror and understand your wounds were made to heal. You have to stare yourself in the eyes and realise this is you in your entirety.

About the author

Cyrus Ahmadnia, the mind behind the Instagram account @papikins is possibly your new favourite writer. Hopefully. Maybe. See you soon.

Cyrus Ahmadnia

Instagram – @papikins

Twitter – @papikinz

Website – www.papikins.com

www.ingramcontent.com/pod-product-compliance
Lightning Source LLC
Chambersburg PA
CBHW021441080526
44588CB00009B/638